RALPH WALDO EMERSON'S

SELF-
RELIANCE

RALPH WALDO EMERSON'S

SELF-RELIANCE

A MODERN-DAY INTERPRETATION
OF A SELF-HELP CLASSIC
BY ANDREW HOLMES

First published in 2010 by
Infinite Ideas Limited
36 St Giles
Oxford, OX1 3LD
United Kingdom
www.infideas.com

A CIP catalogue record for this book is available from the British Library

ISBN 978–1–906821–36–4

Designed and typeset by Cylinder

BRILLIANT IDEAS

INTRODUCTION

Ralph Waldo Emerson's Self-Reliance may be a short essay, but it is packed with advice which is probably more relevant today than it has ever been.

Emerson wrote his essay in the 1840s, and you might think that the kind of things that he was writing about back then would have no relevance to us today. However, when you read it, you can see that many of the societal and personal barriers which prevented people from being self-reliant in nineteenth-century America are similar to those which prevent us from being able to stand on our own two feet today. Of course, there are a few more as well.

We are recovering from the most significant financial collapse since the Wall Street Crash of 1929, and the now-termed Great Recession was the worst economic crisis since the Great Depression. Times are tough for millions of people around the world as the livelihoods on which their financial stability depends have been badly shaken. Economic woes, whether created by contractions in the markets, bad investment decisions or the result of taking on too much debt, can undermine even the most self-reliant of people. But as we enter a new era of austerity and thrift, there is a feeling that we will all become a little bit more self-reliant as a result.

Technology continues to make huge inroads into our daily lives. Having done its job removing our need to do much in the way of manual labour, it is now subsuming office-based work and gradually eliminating routine activities from the workplace. Many people spend their working day in front of a computer screen following processes which are largely driven by software. Others find themselves connected to the workplace 24/7 through increasingly sophisticated mobile technology. Outside of work, the motor car and domestic appliances have changed how we live our lives by making them ever more convenient. Evenings are spent watching television, surfing the net and social networking, not doing endless household chores. All good stuff, of course, but we should recognise the danger of becoming too dependent on technology, as it tends to make us all less self-reliant.

Governments are becoming more, not less, interventionist. The notion of the Nanny State, in which civil servants tell us what we can and cannot do, is undermining our ability to control our own lives and stand on our own two feet. We are bombarded by advice about what is good for us and what is bad, what we should do and what we shouldn't, all of which can prevent us from thinking for ourselves and being in control of our own destiny. In its extreme, the Nanny State erodes our self-reliance and creates a culture of dependency which is not good for the individual or society as a whole.

Emerson wrote Self-Reliance in 1841 – well over 160 years ago – and I believe it provides both a wonderful antidote for the times in which we live and also holds up a beacon with which to guide us. Self-reliance – the ability to stand on our own two feet and live a life which is our own and not borrowed from someone else, or one which is meaningful and not superficial – is essential in establishing our own unique identity. So if, like me, you think self-reliance is important, read on.

1 BELIEVE YOUR OWN THOUGHT

In a world where we are told what to do all the time, it's still important to be able to think for yourself.

DEFINING IDEA...

Everything we do depends for its quality on the thinking we do first.

~ NANCY KLINE, AUTHOR

Emerson starts Self-Reliance by making a reference to some verses written by an eminent painter which he considered to be both original and unconventional. He believed they instilled the sentiment of believing in your own thoughts, something we appear to have great difficulty with today. It often seems that we are told what to do all the time – subliminally, through the advertisements which suggest that if we use a special type of shampoo we'll look better; directly, by the government who like to wrap us up in cotton wool and tell us what we can and cannot do; by our work colleagues, customers and bosses, who bombard us 24/7 with emails and requests.

There seems to be no time to think, perhaps to the extent that being able to think for yourself is becoming a lost art. Too many people are happy to regurgitate what they have read on Wikipedia, or what they have seen or heard on television. Too few value the opportunity to think for themselves and even fewer are capable of original thought or arriving at their own opinion. Historically, of course, there were plenty of people who did just that: philosophers like Aristotle and Plato, scientists like Kepler and Newton, inventors like Da Vinci. All were able to develop insights, unique ideas and were capable of original thinking. Mind you, back then they had the luxury of time and the benefit of peace and quiet; they were not constantly interrupted by yet another pointless email from Simon in accounts or the buzz, buzz of a

BlackBerry. They had time to listen to their thoughts and act on them. Today, however, we find it increasingly difficult to carve out time in which to think – and yet it is so important because it helps to define both who we are and our sense of identity.

Thinking about the world around you in its widest sense helps you become observant and sensitive to what's going on. It opens up your mind to possibilities and helps you develop insight. Although the story may not necessarily be true, we are told that Newton got his ideas about gravitation whilst sitting under an apple tree and watching the fruit fall to the ground. Even if he didn't, we can assume that something must have triggered a thought in his mind – the spark that led him to define the universal laws of gravitation. Thinking is an art because it requires you to listen to your thoughts and then do something with them. It also means being able to ask incisive questions and connect discrete and sometimes unrelated facts and concepts together; those 'what if' questions that have allowed us to advance through the ages. Above all, it requires you to believe your own thought.

HERE'S AN IDEA FOR YOU...

Find somewhere you can think and reflect. It might be the public library or the bottom of your garden. It doesn't matter where, as long as you spend some time thinking and don't forget to take a notebook to jot down your thoughts.

2 BELIEVE WHAT IS TRUE

Each and every one of us has our own world view and this defines how we relate to the world around us.

The poem which may have been the stimulus for Emerson to write Self-Reliance also prompted him to state 'believe what is true for you'. There is a German word which neatly sums this up – weltanschauung. The word is a combination of welt (the world) and anschauung (view) and is a central pillar of German philosophy. It refers to the framework of ideas and beliefs through which we interpret and interact with the world around us.

DEFINING IDEA...

Whether you think that you can, or that you can't, you are usually right.

– HENRY FORD

Our own world view forms as we grow up and is defined by the combination of such things as the country in which we live, our family environment, school, work and so on. It is also defined by our experiences and eventually becomes a powerful tool through which we 'see' the world around us; it forms the core of our belief system. It acts as a lens through which we filter information and the events which we experience, rejecting those things which are not part of our world view and accepting those which are. The beliefs which we hold are in many respects our truths – the things we hold to be true for us and no other. To illustrate just how powerful these can be, we only need to look at what happened to Cortez when he landed in the New World. When he arrived off the coast in 1519 he encountered some fishermen busying themselves about their daily lives. What surprised Cortez was their response – they ignored the huge Spanish galleons which were a few hundred metres from the shore and carried on fishing. They apparently did not 'see' the ships – such vessels were not part of their belief system. In other words, they didn't believe that such things existed; why should they? This demonstrates that we do not so much believe what we see, but see what we believe.

When the Americans and British invaded Iraq for the second time in 2003, there was a huge amount of opposition from politicians and the general public in the UK. People believed that the war was unjust and took to the streets in mass demonstrations. This opposition grew when it became clear that the pretext for the invasion – Saddam Hussein's weapons of mass destruction – never existed. In order to placate the general public in the UK, an inquiry was undertaken which vindicated the government's role and the decision to invade. When Tony Blair was interviewed about the war some time after he had left office, he told reporters that he knew his mind and believed it to be true. In other words, he believed what was true for him – an important quality in any leader. Our world view is clearly important to us because it helps us navigate through our daily lives; however, we do have to be careful not to close off the world around us completely. Otherwise our beliefs may get us into trouble, as perhaps they did Tony Blair.

HERE'S AN IDEA FOR YOU....

What are your core beliefs and universal truths? Write them down and build a picture of your world view. Keep coming back to this note and, each time, consider whether any of your beliefs or truths need to be updated.

3 SPEAK YOUR LATENT CONVICTION

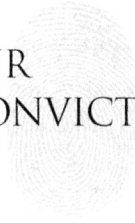

Gut feelings can be very powerful, especially in decision making.

Emerson believed that the ability to give voice to your latent convictions was a universal sense and rather than speak what others think, it is far better to speak what you think. This is all well and good, but we have to be able to listen to our convictions first.

DEFINING IDEA...

*A wise man makes his own decisions;
an ignorant man follows public opinion.*
– CHINESE PROVERB

For example, I am sure everyone knows someone who always seems to make bad decisions. No matter what choices are presented to them, they will always select the one that has the worst possible outcome. Similarly, although perhaps not quite as often, we come across people who are good at decision making. Most of us, however, tend to make a mix of good and bad decisions. So long as the good ones are made when it really counts and we can learn from the bad ones, that's probably all that matters. On further investigation, though, there is more to decision making than meets the eye. After all, despite huge investments in decision-support technologies and information systems which spew out more information than we could ever hope to cope with, the decision-making ability of executives is no better than it has ever been (believe me, I've seen it first hand). The other thing I have noticed is that those people who are good at decision making tend to follow their gut instinct; they don't need fancy technology to tell them what to do because they trust their own judgement. This is exactly what Jack Welch, the well-known

CEO of General Electric, did and it seemed to serve both him and General Electric very well during his leadership.

Jack's ability to listen to his gut feelings is what the author Malcolm Gladwell terms 'thin slicing' in his book Blink. This is all about the power of thinking without thinking; in other words, it's about tuning into gut feelings and speaking your latent convictions. Although the book is a tad repetitive and not quite as good as Gladwell's first book, The Tipping Point – mainly because he keeps coming back to the same example – it does provide a good summary of how our brains are able to process vast amounts of information and arrive at the correct answer almost without conscious effort. The ability to thin slice, or to make snap judgements about people, situations and when solving problems, is something that has been honed ever since we left the primordial soup. It seems that the unconscious mind is a lot more powerful than we give it credit for, so it's time we gave it a bit of space. Next time you need to make a decision and your gut feeling is telling you whether the decision you are about to make is good or bad, try listening to it – because it's more than likely going to be right.

HERE'S AN IDEA FOR YOU...

Often you find that your initial view on something is correct, so tune into your latent judgement skills. Give yourself time to let your brain process all the available information and make its judgement. You'll also notice that you'll 'feel' it, so tune into what your body is telling you as well.

4 DETECT AND WATCH THAT GLEAM OF LIGHT

Ideas are the lifeblood of an organisation and are central to creativity. But how do we capture them?

DEFINING IDEA...

Invention is 1% inspiration and 99% perspiration.
~ THOMAS EDISON

Emerson was someone who was fascinated by the behaviours and actions of the people around him, and especially those in authority. He was also a bit negative and seemed to go off on one every now and then. Reading Self-Reliance sometimes feels as though he had an axe to grind but, then again, he had to push home his point. He believed that self-reliance extended to every facet of life and not, for example, just to earning a living. He was clear that we should rely on our own unique qualities rather than looking to others for opinions or ideas. He believed that we should learn to appreciate and act upon our own flashes of inspiration rather than focus too heavily on those made by others – 'bards and sages' in his time, or celebrities in ours. This is fine, but I think he was missing the point. We all have our unique set of talents and it is nice to appreciate those which we don't possess. For example, I recently visited the Louvre and saw some wonderful paintings; things I could never paint, but could still appreciate.

However, we should consider the subtext of what Emerson is saying here, as this short part of his essay can be considered as a call to arms for innovation and ideas. Although every one of us has ideas and flashes of inspiration, I wonder just how many act upon them. Most ideas just float by with little more than a cursory glance, never to be recaptured again. What separates those among us who can be considered to be innovative from those who cannot is not so much that the innovators have more ideas than the average person, but that they are better at recognising them for what they are and doing something with them. Famous inventors like Edison, Ford and, more recently, James Dyson are clearly able to do this.

As individuals, it's comparatively easy to discipline ourselves to recognise the flashes of inspiration which occur from time to time. It can be a lot harder for organisations. They have to deal with broader issues, such as profitability, financial stability and the markets. And then there is internal politics, which can kill even the brightest of ideas. However, most organisations recognise that innovation is central to long-term success and build processes around the capture, assessment and commercialisation of ideas. Being successful means that they have to accept that there are some who, like Edison and Dyson, are better at coming up with ideas than the average employee. If they want to survive in an increasingly cut-throat market, they have to do their best to give creative types the space they need.

HERE'S AN IDEA FOR YOU...

Like most people, I'm certain you have plenty of ideas. Instead of letting them float by, keep a pad at your side at all times and whenever you get a flash of inspiration, jot it down. You can review it later and then decide what to do with it. At least you will have captured it, which is an excellent start.

5 IN EVERY WORK OF GENIUS WE RECOGNISE OUR OWN REJECTED THOUGHTS

How many times do you think 'I could have done that'?

DEFINING IDEA...

The ideas I use are mostly the ideas of people who don't develop them.

~ THOMAS EDISON

Having addressed our failure to recognise and act on our flashes of inspiration, Emerson goes on to rub salt in the wound by reminding us just how bad we feel when other people act on similar ideas to our own or have opinions which we were unwilling to express ourselves. As he says, 'In every work of genius we recognize our own rejected thoughts: they come to us with a certain alienated majesty. Great works of art have no more affecting lesson than this. They teach us to abide by our spontaneous impression with good-humoured inflexibility then most when the whole cry of voices is on the other side. Else, to-morrow a stranger will say with masterly good sense precisely what we have thought and felt all the time, and we shall be forced to take with shame our own opinion from another.'

An apocryphal story which illustrates this quite well involved a young girl walking round an art gallery with her father. When they came to a room which was adorned on every side by huge canvasses which had been painted purple, the daughter turned to her father and said, 'Dad, anyone can do that,' to which he replied, 'Of course they can – but he did.' Kind of sums it up.

When I got the idea to write my first humour book, Pains on Trains, I contacted some publishers and persuaded one to publish it. It was quite a departure from the type of thing I had written before, but it was a lot of fun. I am not for one moment suggesting that it was a work of genius, but I did receive at least a dozen messages from people who read the book. Amongst these were a few letters from people who explained to me that they'd had a similar idea for a book but, for whatever reason, never pursued it. They either believed that nobody would publish it or felt writing it was beyond their ability. Although they were delighted that I had, you could feel the pang of sorrow which they felt because they hadn't followed their idea through to fruition. Still, it didn't stop them from telling me about their experiences on the trains and offering new anecdotes should the book ever be revised!

It seems that it's just too easy to summarily reject our thoughts and ideas, only to be disappointed when someone else comes up with the same idea and does something with it, or expresses an opinion which is identical to ours. It happens all the time and we have to accept that it is quite natural for people to have similar ideas to our own. It's a bit like the simultaneous development of the light bulb or the motor car or even the atomic bomb; sometimes the environment creates the conditions for people to have similar insights. Then it's all about who does something with it first.

HERE'S AN IDEA FOR YOU...

The next time you have a great idea (and jotted it down, as I suggested in the previous chapter), don't reject it out of hand; instead, think about what you'd have to do to bring it alive. It's too easy to dismiss it; learn not to do so.

6 ENVY IS IGNORANCE

As one of the seven deadly sins, envy is often considered the worst of them all; it screws you up.

Emerson believed that each and every one of us comes to the same conclusion that envy is ignorance. Although he never explained what he meant by this, I think we can understand the subtext. Envy stops us from focusing on what we want to achieve for ourselves. It forces us to be who we aren't and prevents us from realising our full potential. Envy is more like a ball and chain holding us back and stunting our personal growth.

DEFINING IDEA...

Our envy of others devours us most of all.
– ALEXANDER SOLZHENITSYN

Envy is universal, of that we can be certain; otherwise it would have never been included as one of the seven deadly sins. It also appears in the Bible as one of the Ten Commandments: 'Thou shalt not covet thy neighbour's house, thou shalt not covet thy neighbour's wife, nor his manservant, nor his maidservant, nor his ox, nor his ass, nor any thing that is thy neighbour's.' As a sin, it is often believed to be the worst of the lot because it has this terrible habit of eating away at you and can lead to many of the others. The problem is that everyone suffers from it from time to time and for some it is a constant force in their lives: you know the type, the middle-class social climbers who want to appear more important and influential than they actually are, or could ever be. They spend their lives coveting the possessions and success of others and as a result never live an authentic life themselves.

Envy lies at the heart of the media-obsessed culture in which we now live, with its seemingly unending fixation with celebrities. For many, celebrity offers a shortcut to success, fame and wealth which is why when you ask teenagers what they want to be when they grow up, many can only offer you 'fame' or 'celebrity'. Fuelled by daytime television, glossy magazines and talent shows, it's no wonder that everyone wants what celebrities have got. But do they also want the constant media attention, the drugs, the depression, the car crashes that are celebrity love lives and having every minute of their daily existence on full display? I'm sure many don't. Wealth and status also lead to a lot of envy and the self-destructive behaviours that go with it. Sure, I would love to be as wealthy as a hedge-fund manager, but I sure as hell won't be living like one on my income. But that hasn't stopped millions from over-extending themselves, buying the McMansions and living a lifestyle that they patently can't afford, only for it all to come crashing down with the credit crunch. Perhaps we have to be of a certain age to realise it, and maybe also sufficiently comfortable in our own skin not to feel envious of anything or anyone.

HERE'S AN IDEA FOR YOU...

The next time you feel the pang of envy consider why you feel that way. Seek to rewire your brain to avoid the 'I wish I was like…' or 'I wish I had…' thoughts that lie at the heart of envy. Focus on what you have and what you want to achieve for you, and not wanting what others have.

7 IMITATION IS SUICIDE

Imitation smacks of unoriginality and suppresses your true self.

When Emerson stated that imitation was suicide, I'm sure he meant it in the existential sense rather than literally. In today's media-rich world it is easy to imitate other people, and especially celebrities whose lives are lived in the public eye. And because they seem to have everything – money, fame, love and so on – it's no wonder that the youth of today would rather emulate Paris Hilton than develop their own, unique identity which takes hard work and plenty of self-awareness. But why would you want to? Why wouldn't you want to be who you are, to have an identity which is uniquely you?

DEFINING IDEA...

It is better to fail in originality than to succeed in imitation.
~ HERMAN MELVILLE

If imitation prevents you from being who you truly are then it is indeed suicide, because it not only stops you from understanding what really makes you tick, but also prevents you from experiencing a life which is uniquely yours. Those who choose to imitate also end up developing strange associations with the people they worship, and we see this in the massive outpourings of grief when famous people like Princess Diana and Michael Jackson die. I have to admit that I find it all somewhat strange, and I'm sure Emerson would too.

In the 1992 movie Single White Female, a young woman's flatmate (who had answered an ad in the paper – hence the title of the film) starts to imitate her. It begins quite harmlessly with the flatmate borrowing the woman's clothes, but it doesn't take long before she begins to look and behave just like her. Over the course of the film, things get progressively worse (as you'd expect) with the flatmate killing sundry people, including the woman's ex-boyfriend. Fortunately the flatmate gets what she deserves… in the end. Of course that was a film, but sometimes life can be stranger than fiction. One example involved a fan of Jennifer Lopez who so desperately wanted to look like her that he had a sex change and plastic surgery. The 23-year-old man underwent hormone treatment, breast enlargements, buttock implants and face sculpturing in order to look the spitting image of Ms Lopez (apparently he was a little disappointed with the size of his breasts, which weren't big enough). Although some, but thankfully few, people go to such extreme lengths to imitate those they worship, imitation is all around us. We see it in the fake goods which sell for a fraction of the price of the originals, like Louis Vuitton bags and Rolex watches, as well as the way women choose to dress in the same clothes as their favourite celebrities. The reason why this is so prevalent is because it is so easy – easy to appear rich, easy to look like a celebrity and easy to be someone you are not. The problem, though, is that it is unoriginal.

HERE'S AN IDEA FOR YOU…

It's fine to like TV or pop stars, but it's dangerous to want to become like them. To prevent yourself from drifting into imitation territory sit down with a piece of blank paper and write down what uniquely defines you as a person. Seek to emphasis your uniqueness in your daily life so that you live your life, not someone else's.

8 HE MUST TAKE HIMSELF FOR BETTER, FOR WORSE

The American nation is a wonderful yardstick for resilience and ability to pick yourself up after a fall.

DEFINING IDEA...

America is a vast conspiracy to make you happy.

~ JOHN UPDIKE

Emerson lived at a time of immense importance to the young United States. He was born at the turn of the nineteenth century, just a few short years after the end of the War of Independence, and died before the American empire finally emerged in the early part of the twentieth century. During these early years, people like Emerson mattered because they provided an essential contribution to American identity. Indeed, his boundless self-confidence and optimism was the very thing needed for the young nation. For example, he was instrumental in getting American intellectuals to join the mainstream world and building the basis for a national body of literature. During this period he wrote extensively on topics as wide-ranging as friendship and the nature of experience. As the US grew into a fully fledged global power, it inevitably had to deal with the ups and downs you would associate with any emerging nation, not least the civil war which tore the country apart. Emerson witnessed these, and it is clear that such events affected his writing in many different ways. More than anything, though, it was the self-reliance and resilience that was and still is highly infectious – and which is well encapsulated in the 'American dream'.

America's ability to bounce back is instructive and in many respects is akin to the entrepreneur who is always willing to give something a try and then, after it has all turned to dust, try again. Without the yoke of history which Europe has, America, more than any other nation, is able to reinvent itself time after time and is expert at putting the past behind it and moving on after periods of difficulty. It did it after the Great Depression and is doing it again after the financial collapse of 2007. Such resilience in the face of adversity – the Blitz Spirit if you like – is an inbuilt part of the American psyche. Maybe it's because they have so little history to fall back on. More likely it has to do with the national culture which, if you think about it, was born out of adversity and taking risks.

One aspect which is particularly interesting is how failure is perceived. Unlike in Europe, and especially the United Kingdom, where people who fail in business are usually treated as pariahs, they are often considered heroes in the US. The businessman who has given something a go but failed is not seen as a failure per se in the States, but as someone who has taken a few risks and not opted for the safe path (the frontier spirit has always been part of America). In Europe, businesspeople can be crushed by the experience, but Americans are energised by it. They do not perceive it as a failure, but part and parcel of taking a few chances and as just a stumbling block along the way. We can all learn something from this attitude.

HERE'S AN IDEA FOR YOU...

How do you deal with failure or the little upsets that occur from time to time? Instead of viewing them as major catastrophes and reasons not to take a risk or two, consider them as 'little learns' which tell you something about yourself and what you are trying to achieve.

9 IT'S ALWAYS BETTER TO EARN YOUR LIVING

Easy money is easily lost – and easily wasted.

Emerson was someone who believed in the Protestant work ethic. Although
he believed the universe was full of good, he felt that none of us deserved
what we hadn't worked for. Getting something for nothing always came with
problems – a lesson we need to reflect on today.

DEFINING IDEA...

*You have to earn money the hard
way. Because no-one will serve it up
to you on a silver platter.*
– GORDON WU, ENTREPRENEUR

As the financial system recently went
into its massive swoon, it took many
economists and politicians by surprise.
Apart from a very small number of
analysts who could see it coming, the
majority believed the problems would be temporary. How wrong they
were. Once they knew it was going to be a lot worse than anyone had
anticipated, they swung into action and poured money into the markets
at rates unheard of. As banks which were too big to fail were bailed out,
hundreds of billions were doled out by governments across the world in
an attempt to limit the impact of the collapse. As a result we may have
avoided another Great Depression, but we have loaded ourselves with such
massive amounts of debt that we're still going to pass through a lengthy
period of economic pain.

Naturally, we are probably delighted (at least now) that governments did
step in to tackle the crisis, but all this 'free money' that is swilling around is
already causing a few issues. For example, the bosses of the big automobile
companies flew to Washington in individual private jets to claim their

share of the bailout fund and investment and retail banks have used the cash dished out to them to pay outlandish bonuses to their staff.

Such poor behaviour comes as no surprise to Bill Bonner, the author of financial and economic texts including *Financial Reckoning Day: Surviving the Soft Depression of the 21st Century and Empire of Debt*. Bill isn't a great fan of bailouts and believes that they are, in fact, very dangerous. In his mind, without the sweat of honest toil on it, easy money is almost worse than none at all. It seems that throwing free money at a problem rarely works; it didn't work for the Romans when they increased the money supply in the first century AD, and it failed to help the Spanish when they discovered a mountain of silver in Peru which they mined, flooding Spain with silver coins in the sixteenth century. You see, when money comes all too easily, you end up forgetting its true worth – just like the lottery winner who fritters the cash away and ends up bankrupt. The same is true of government stimuli, which is why we are seeing banks and others blowing their 'free cash'. After all, it's so much easier to spend other people's money than your own. In any case, how can you be self-reliant if you're dependent on the largesse of someone else?

HERE'S AN IDEA FOR YOU...

One of the games I like to play is to imagine how a massive lottery win affects people; give it a try. What would you do if you never had to earn money again? Would you get bored, waste the money or use it sensibly? Could you handle a big stimulus or are you someone who would rather earn your millions?

10 YOU'LL NEVER KNOW UNTIL YOU'VE TRIED

It's easy to make excuses about why you can't do something, but far harder to just give it a go.

Emerson believed that the only person who really knows what you could do is you. And, more importantly, that the only way you could know was to give something a go. In other words, only after you have tried something and immersed yourself in it, could you truly say whether or not you could do it. This makes enormous sense and once you have tried something and succeeded, or at the very least learned from the process, you should be more confident in your own abilities.

DEFINING IDEA...

Either you let your life slip away by not doing the things you want to do, or you get up and do them.
~ ROGER VON OECH, AUTHOR AND PRESIDENT OF CREATIVE THINK

Naturally, all of us harbour fears about what we can and cannot do; it's part of being human. Some are legitimate, like the fear of dying if you were to BASE jump off Angel Falls (and the fact that people do such mad things may have more to do with chemical imbalances in the brain than any latent desire to face their fears). Crazy people aside, most of us fear all kinds of non-life-threatening things such as making public presentations, going for the next promotion, moving jobs or even trying out a new hobby. Much of the fear relates to our concern that we might fail in the endeavour and as a result we don't bother trying or give up at the first obstacle. The sad thing is that such fears hold us back.

We are also held in check by what other people say: the critics around us like our parents, friends, colleagues and bosses, who pour scorn on new ventures or believe they know more about us than we do. If you listen to internal and external critics long enough, you end up believing them and develop self-limiting behaviours which act as permanent barriers to personal growth.

Applying the techniques of neuro-linguistic programming (NLP) is one way in which you can tackle your personal limitations. One NLP course I went on a while ago focused on the power of limiting beliefs. Like most courses, this one used a range of techniques to both illustrate how we hold ourselves back and show how to break through to peak performance. One exercise in particular sticks out, even today, and involved breaking a wooden arrow, complete with metal tip, on my neck. Naturally, I didn't expect to break it; in fact, I fully anticipated spending some time in A&E – but I was willing to give it a go because of its symbolism. There I was, standing with the arrow poised on my neck waiting for the instructor to push and snap it. And, after a few agonising seconds, he did. I didn't end up with an arrow through my neck, but I did feel more confident as a result. If I could do that, surely I could do anything.

HERE'S AN IDEA FOR YOU...

The next time you feel you might be holding yourself back, try flicking the switch. Instead of associating pain with doing something you are fearful of and pleasure with avoiding it, switch your thinking so that you associate pleasure with doing it and pain with avoiding it. It's incredibly motivating.

11 DO YOUR BEST

Measuring achievement is of course important, but shouldn't we measure effort too?

DEFINING IDEA...

No man fails who does his best.

~ ORISON SWETT MARDEN, PROLIFIC AUTHOR
OF SUCCESS AND MOTIVATION BOOKS

Emerson believed that anyone who had put their heart and soul into their work and had done their very best could hold their head up high. Merely talking about it or only putting in a modicum of effort wasn't good enough in his mind; it was all or nothing. He believed that doing your best was an admirable quality and that although you might not always be successful, knowing that you had done all you could was often all that mattered; at least you could look yourself in the eye. This ethos is central to many youth movements such as the Scouts and Guides, and is a great philosophy for life in general. Indeed, doing your absolute best in everything you do is something that we should all aspire to, and it doesn't matter if it's at school, university, work or home.

If you think about it, doing your best is also central to self-reliance because it allows you not only to test your capabilities, but also helps you to learn and therefore extend them. It's only when you are at the edge of your ability that you can really test your mettle and see just how much you can depend on yourself. Only ever working inside your comfort zone, or doing just enough to get by, may be easy but is rarely rewarding. And it never allows you to develop into a fully rounded person or realise your full potential.

One thing we can take away from our time at school is the way in which we were appraised. Although achievement was important, so was effort and it was this that measured just how much of our heart and soul we put into our studies. We may not always have got the grades we wanted, but it showed that we had tried. I, for one, always knew what mattered when my report came home – effort. It's a shame we don't have a similar measurement system at work, as this would allow organisations to identify the true stars who put their heart and soul into their work, and who therefore want the company to succeed.

The following quote from Theodore Roosevelt sums up the essence of Emerson's point: 'It is not the critic who counts, nor the man who points out how the strong man stumbled or where the doer of deeds could have done better. The credit belongs to the man who is actually in the arena; whose face is marred by dust and sweat and blood; who strives valiantly; who errs and comes up short again and again; who knows the great enthusiasms, the great devotions, and spends himself in a worthy cause; who at the best knows in the end triumph of high achievement; and who at worst, if he fails while daring greatly; so that his place shall never be with those cold and timid souls who know neither defeat or victory.'

HERE'S AN IDEA FOR YOU...

When you are working on your next task, give it your full concentration and really put the effort in to produce the best possible end result. Even if it doesn't lead to glittering success, you should be proud of yourself for doing your very best.

12 TRUST THYSELF

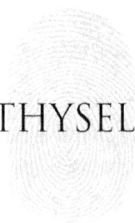

If you can't trust those around you, you have to at least be able to trust yourself.

Emerson believed that every heart vibrates to that iron string. Well, most – but not all, it seems.

We are living in a time where trust is an essential but seemingly disappearing commodity. We have seen politicians claiming expenses that were in no way legitimate, CEOs using their businesses as personal piggybanks and conmen like Bernie Madoff taking investors' money and spending it on themselves. When we hear of such appalling behaviour we cannot be blamed for thinking that society is breaking down. After all, losing trust means losing faith in one of the basic mechanisms that holds a fully functioning society together. And until such time as it's repaired, it doesn't matter what politicians might say – they have broken too many promises themselves for us to believe them, and their actions do not marry up with their words. In a world where everyone is suspicious, you have to be able to trust yourself.

But what does 'trust thyself' mean in practice? I think it means having trust in your own capabilities and knowledge and being willing to rely on your latent skills and abilities to get things done. Isn't that what self-reliance is all about? The problem, though, is that there is this thing called the inner game.

The inner game has been popularised by Timothy Gallwey, who developed the idea as a sports coach. Simply, the inner game is about the internal conversations that occur in your head between what Gallwey terms Self 1 and Self 2. Self 1 is the stern know-it-all who issues commands and judges the results, the inner conversation that says 'you haven't finished this yet' or 'I'm not sure if this is a good idea'. Self 1 is generally untrusting of Self 2. Self 2 is the human being itself, packed with natural potential as well as the skills and capabilities to achieve most things. Our ability to rely on ourselves and continue to develop and realise our potential depends heavily on our ability to limit the controlling Self 1, allowing Self 2 to carry out the tasks in hand in a calm and natural manner. Gallwey noticed this during coaching sessions with tennis players and, later, with golfers. By focusing the judgemental Self 1 on a component of the ball, such as its speed, he found that a player's Self 2 would take over and make a perfect hit; turning down or distracting Self 1 was key to success. This is similar to the state of flow that we sometimes reach when we are so focused on a task that time flies and we seem to tackle it effortlessly. The inner game is an excellent way to interpret and ultimately manage your internal dialogue and develop that self-trust that we increasingly need to rely on.

HERE'S AN IDEA FOR YOU...

I'm sure you have your inner voice, niggling away at you when you do things. Try to apply Gallwey's ideas to what you do; it doesn't matter whether this is work related or a sport. See if you can distract your untrusting Self 1 so that Self 2 can get on with the task.

13 HE GIVES AN INDEPENDENT, GENUINE VERDICT

Although we like to dismiss them, there is something quite pure about young people. They have yet to conform.

Although we often dismiss youth and youth culture, Emerson could see that, out of everyone, young people are those who are able to see the world for what it is. And because they are unencumbered they are able to express their opinions without any need to wrap them up so that they are palatable for their audience. This is, of course, what adults (and parents in particular) struggle with.

DEFINING IDEA...

Greatness is the dream of youth realised in old age.
~ ALFRED DE VIGNY, FRENCH WRITER

Emerson was someone who never dismissed youth, as in his mind young people conformed to no one because they were unconquered. I see it in my son Tom, who is in his late teens. When he expresses any opinion it is delivered with such surety and belief that you'd think he had total knowledge and that no one could tell him anything new. In his mind, his opinion is the right one and everyone else's is wrong. And although there are times when his view of the world is perhaps too purist and simplistic, there are times where his insight is not only incisive but also shows how conforming to the norms of society makes us adults blind to what is going around us.

One night, a few years ago, I finished work quite late. As I walked onto the Strand in central London, I came upon a demonstration by a large number of students. The street was lined by policemen, and as I walked along it I watched the students marching by to a samba beat with their placards waving.

Before I knew it, I was being bundled aside by a burly copper who told me to get out of the way. There was me, in my suit and tie, being pushed about by the policemen as the demonstrators went past. The irony was not lost on me. The other thing that went through my mind was that give these students a few years and they would be where I was – doing what society wants us to do, conforming.

Pick any period you like and you will be able to identify a youth culture that shocked the establishment of the time. Whether it was the Flappers in the 1920s – the new breed of young women who wore short skirts, bobbed their hair and listened to jazz – or the Mods and Rockers of the 1960s who used to knock seven bells out of each other on Brighton Beach, or the punks of the late 70s who loved angry music and prided themselves on being anti-establishment, or the Hoodies of the 2000s who skulk about shopping centres, each did what they set out to do and that was to push back against convention and the accepted norms of behaviour at the time. This was their last roll of the dice before they had to grow up and become adults – and we should cut them some slack.

HERE'S AN IDEA FOR YOU...

If you have children, try not to dismiss their views out of hand. Tempting though it is to show them who the adult is, stop and listen to what they have to say. Some of their views may actually make you think and re-evaluate your own opinions.

14 BUT THE MAN IS, AS IT WERE, CLAPPED INTO JAIL BY HIS CONSCIOUSNESS

As adults, it's a sad fact that as soon as we express an opinion, we feel unable to change it.

One of the central thrusts of Self-Reliance is about having the courage of your convictions and being able to stand up and be counted. Emerson took a dim view of those around him who were unwilling to say what they really thought. But, by the same token, he recognised that once you entered adulthood the ease with which you could change your opinion was much more difficult, if not impossible, to achieve. It was, as he quite aptly stated, as if you had become trapped by your own consciousness.

DEFINING IDEA...

He that never changes his opinions, never corrects his mistakes, will never be wiser on the morrow than he is today.
~ TRYON EDWARDS, US THEOLOGIAN

Observant as ever, Emerson saw the problems of speaking your mind and sharing your opinion, and there are those people who will love you for it and those who will hate you. This rather makes it a 'damned if you do, damned if you don't' bind. Even though you may like to conveniently forget your opinion, those around you are more than happy to remind you of it at every opportunity. This is what politicians like to term the 'court of public opinion', which for them is a great way of either maintaining their position or changing with the wind. Of course, for politicians the only time the supposed court of public opinion ever gets a chance to express a view is during an election, by which time most people have forgotten what they were expressing an opinion about…

Politicians aside, Emerson's observation explains a lot, particularly why some people never want to give an opinion about anything and others refuse to budge once they have set their mind on things. Both are far from ideal. The person who refuses to give an opinion might as well not exist; they never show the world who they are and what they stand for. Equally, those who refuse to change their point of view tend to be perceived as intransigent and bigoted.

So what can we do to ensure that we offer our opinions freely, but are also willing and open-minded enough to change them in light of new information? It's actually comparatively easy. First, sharing your opinion freely means not worrying about what other people might think. We often hold back because we're concerned that our opinion might be rubbished or laughed at – but an opinion is just that; it isn't a universal truth, nor is it a hard fact, and what's more it's as valid as the next guy's. Keeping an open mind is also quite simple and requires that you try new things on a regular basis, read books or articles that you wouldn't normally and try out new hobbies or sports from time to time. This ensures that you're receptive to new information and helps you become less wedded to existing ideas and more willing to change them.

HERE'S AN IDEA FOR YOU...

Training yourself to be more open-minded means doing different things. So the next time you're driving home from work, take a different route. The next time you pick up your usual newspaper, take one which expresses a different political point of view. These things are easy to do, but powerful, so give it a go.

15 SINKING LIKE DARTS INTO THE EARS OF MEN

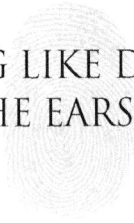

Telling it how it is may not always be easy, but there are times when we absolutely have to do it.

Emerson believed that anyone who was able to provide unbiased views and opinions was formidable. In his mind such individuals were unaffected by the politics and behaviours that lead to bias and had the ability to observe the world around them with an almost childlike innocence. Not only are such observations accurate, but they are also exceptionally powerful. He also recognised that such people were few and far between, which rather explains why he considered them formidable.

DEFINING IDEA...

Face reality as it is, not as it was or as you wish it were.

– JACK WELCH, FORMER CEO OF GENERAL ELECTRIC

The ability to speak our mind and share our opinions freely becomes more difficult as we move from childhood to adulthood, as we've seen. We also shouldn't forget that the positional power of those around us together with our own self-consciousness act as barriers to telling it how it is. Hans Christian Andersen's story of the emperor's new clothes sums up this exceptionally well. Despite being hoodwinked by a couple of crooks, the emperor's closest advisors would not tell their ruler that his supposed new clothes did not exist and that he was, in fact, stark naked. As he processed through the streets everyone believed the same and it was only when a child shouted out that the emperor was naked that people agreed. The boy said what everyone was no doubt thinking but were unwilling, for whatever reason, to point out.

Despite the difficulties we have in telling it how it is, sometimes it is sorely needed. At a personal level it might be telling someone you love about an annoying habit, or telling your child that what they are doing is not a good idea and will have long-term consequences. If it's difficult to achieve at the personal level, you can begin to see why it is even harder in an organisation. Those who see that things have to change, or who are willing to point out bad and wrong-headed behaviour, do their companies a major service. It is a real shame, however, that they are often persecuted. Whistleblowers, in particular, have a very bad time of it and often have to turn to the courts to protect them. Fortunately, many companies are introducing anonymous reporting systems which help people to bring issues to the attention of the board. Where it really matters, though, is at the political level. Here all we want is for our leaders to call it out and not give us platitudes or deliver the news in such a roundabout way that the message is lost. From time to time, we do get leaders who are able to speak for the nation – Franklin Roosevelt, Winston Churchill and Barack Obama are just three examples.

Tough love, as it's called, is something we all have to demonstrate from time to time, and sometimes you just have to be cruel to be kind.

HERE'S AN IDEA FOR YOU...

The next time you need to deliver a home truth, don't shy away from it. First, consider what the message is. Next, prepare it and if necessary rehearse it in your mind or out loud. Finally, try to understand how the other person will react and prepare yourself for the inevitable reaction.

16 THESE ARE THE VOICES WE HEAR IN SOLITUDE

Although we might look externally for answers, very often we can figure them out for ourselves.

DEFINING IDEA...

Everyone who wills can hear the inner voice. It is within everyone.

– GANDHI

When Emerson addresses the topic of speaking the truth and expressing opinion, he suggests that for the most part we tend to do this privately. Although our inner voice is with us all of the time, it's at its most lucid when we're on our own. When we are not distracted, it is as loud as it is clear but, as Emerson points out, as soon as we enter the world again the inner voice becomes much, much fainter and is drowned out and typically ignored. As someone who was apt to express his inner voice, you get the sense that he was disappointed that so many of us fail to both listen to and act upon the advice which the inner voice gives us. Unfortunately, he failed to give his readers any hints or tips about how best to exploit it, which is a shame but not unsurprising. A lot more is known about the brain now, and there has been much more interest in such things as the subconscious mind than there was back then.

The inner voice can be considered to be the mouthpiece of the subconscious and your very own supercomputer. We tend to forget just how powerful the brain is as we busy ourselves throughout the day. Most of us use very little of its total processing power: in fact, it's thought that the average person uses perhaps as little as 10% of their brain's capacity at any one time. It's clear that no one uses 100% either, and despite the various debates about how much of the grey stuff we actually use, it is evident that we could use a lot more than we actually do.

There is no doubt that this is becoming much harder due to advances in technology which are making us all increasingly distracted and less able to concentrate or focus. That's bad news for the inner voice, because we end up failing to give it time to do what it's really good at – processing information, generating realistic answers and arriving at a solution, something which the Internet or your iPhone isn't.

I'm a great fan of allowing my subconscious mind to do the hard work for me. Whenever I find myself facing a difficult or interesting challenge, I don't attempt to get everything sorted out straight away; I let it soak in my mind. I park the idea or problem in my head and usually after a few days an answer sort of pops out. I am so used to it now that I trust my inner voice and subconscious mind to come up with the answer, whatever I do. Sometimes I have to exercise a little patience, as it's not always as quick as I would like it to be, but it has yet to let me down. Give it a try.

HERE'S AN IDEA FOR YOU...

If you need to come up with an answer to a problem which appears to be almost impossible to solve, don't try to resolve it then and there. One of the best things you can do is sleep on it and let your subconscious mind get to work.

17 SOCIETY EVERYWHERE

The 'Nanny State' seems to be looking out for us, but in reality it undermines our self-reliance.

When Emerson made the statement that 'society everywhere is conspiring against the manhood of every one of its members,' I'm sure he didn't mean it in the literal sense. His beef was more general in nature and was directed at the loss of self-reliance that came with complying with the expectations and demands of the state, which tended to override those of the general public. Although we need our governments to set some basic rules by which we all live, it often seems that things have got just a little out of hand nowadays. For some reason, governments have decided that we can no longer be trusted to look after ourselves as we're unable to eat properly, sneeze into a handkerchief or know what's good for us. They seem to have invaded every part of our lives with advice, rules and regulations which at best are nothing more than common sense and at worst are nonsensical and even highly damaging.

DEFINING IDEA...

Preconceived notions are the locks on the door to wisdom.
~ MERRY BROWNE, AUTHOR

The results speak for themselves. Children, for example, are no longer always allowed to play in the playground, wear ties or scarves (they could be dangerous, you see) or do what kids should do – such as get dirty, make camps and play with abandon in the fields. I used to spend hours building camps in my local woods and playing on farms, and although I used to get the occasional cut and often ended up bruised, it was fun and mind-expanding stuff. Today, kids aren't officially allowed to do much at all because of the supposed risk, and as a result are often wrapped up in cotton wool and kept on a tight leash by their now overly concerned parents. Even adults can often feel disempowered in a world where they are, according to the government, surrounded by risk. If you listened to all the advice given to you, you wouldn't drink, eat, or do much else; it seems that danger lurks at every turn. What you have to remember is that many of the risks which are identified by the state are often nothing more than an immediate reaction to incomplete information.

Such nannying is bad for all of us for three reasons. First, it engenders a culture of dependency in which people feel disempowered and unable to think for themselves. Over time they increasingly expect the state to do things for them and advise them on what they should and shouldn't do, which crushes free thinking. Second, it creates a culture of fear, where quite normal, everyday risks are blown out of all proportion. Third, and most importantly, it undermines self-reliance. I recommend that you learn not to take all official advice at face value. Consider the research or statistics which support it and decide just how reliable it is before you act. It's unfortunate, but much of it is quite flimsy and acting on it without thinking isn't always wise.

HERE'S AN IDEA FOR YOU...

If you have children, help them understand and explain to them the importance of questioning and assessing official advice in a rational way. This will then help them to become self-reliant adults.

18 IT LOVES NOT REALITIES AND CREATORS, BUT NAMES AND CUSTOMS

Traditions are important because they keep us in touch with the past, but that doesn't mean we should follow them slavishly.

Emerson viewed society as a joint-stock company in 'which its members agree, for the better securing of his bread to each shareholder, to surrender the liberty and culture of the eater'. As such, conformity and tradition were more important than self-reliance and independence. So I think we can be certain that he wasn't a fan, given that the focus of his essay was self-reliance.

DEFINING IDEA...

Tradition is an explanation for acting without thinking.
– GRACE MCGARVIE,
US POLITICAL SCIENTIST

Although perhaps a little too harsh, Emerson had a point – tradition, which in effect means doing the same thing over and over again without question, tends to crush new thinking. We only need to look to history to see how tradition is capable of preventing progress. Here's an example. Until Copernicus suggested otherwise in 1543, the received wisdom – since Ptolemy – was that the Earth was at the centre of our solar system, and the other planets and sun revolved around it. Because the church held the traditional Ptolemaic view, it was never willing to accept any alternatives. In fact, so entrenched were they that anyone who opposed official doctrine was branded a heretic, and with this came the risk of, at least, the destruction of your reputation or, at worst, a death sentence. No wonder that Copernicus didn't publish his ideas until he was on his deathbed, deliberately designed to avoid the persecution of the church. Galileo supported Copernicus's views and was, however, willing to go out on a limb; as a result he was sent to trial.

Unsurprisingly, he was found guilty and had to spend the rest of his life under house arrest.

Although tradition can be a bad thing, especially when it's no longer capable of adding value to an organisation or a society, it does serve a couple of useful purposes. The first is keeping some of our history alive and the second is instilling some discipline into people's lives. Both are important, although in quite different ways. Keeping some traditions alive shows that we still have a link to the past and a sense of identity. For instance, traditions such as the opening of Parliament or the annual burning of effigies of Guy Fawkes (and sometimes the Pope) help to hold onto those things which make the English truly English. In an increasingly globalised world, it's no wonder that traditions which provide unique cultural identity are increasingly important and, indeed, encouraged.

Tradition also allows us to maintain some basic disciplines. Small though it is, the family meal in which everyone sits down at the same time and eats together is important. Not only does it help to maintain some basic table manners, but it gives everyone a chance to talk about what they have done during the day. And what is encouraging is that it's coming back into vogue after years of decline, and we are all getting better at the art of communication as a result.

HERE'S AN IDEA FOR YOU...

Make a list of traditions for both the place where you live and your family. As you make your list consider what purpose they serve. Are there any which are no longer useful and are there any you think are needed but which don't appear on your list?

19 WHOSO WOULD BE A MAN MUST BE A NONCONFORMIST

One of the biggest challenges we all face is whether or not we can stand up for who we are.

DEFINING IDEA...

The Non-Conformist Conscience makes cowards of us all.

~ MAX BEERBOHM

In Emerson's opinion, the only way a person could be considered a man (or woman, of course) was if they refused to follow the herd. In other words, he believed that you had to be a nonconformist in order to demonstrate to the world that you stood for something. It's true that in order to stand out from the crowd you have to do something which most people wouldn't – and although we can all think of famous sports stars or perhaps celebrities who have skills we do not, Emerson wasn't really referring to them. Instead he was focused on those people in society who were willing to challenge the received wisdom and norms of behaviour of the day and put themselves on the line as a result. They were the true nonconformists and they are few and far between. But we have all heard of them, people like Leonardo Da Vinci, Martin Luther and Emmeline Pankhurst. They were willing to challenge the orthodoxy of their time and, more importantly, stand their ground no matter what the risk.

One of the most inspiring was Mahatma Gandhi, who was instrumental in bringing India its independence. His early life was pretty nondescript; he studied law in England and travelled to South Africa. However, it was how he was treated there that changed everything – he was thrown off a train and beaten by a stagecoach driver for refusing to make way for Europeans, and also refused board and lodging. These events allowed him to see first hand the injustices meted out to non-whites and as a result of his experiences he decided to help the Indians in defying the Transvaal government. This resulted in more beatings as well as a prison sentence. After seven years in South Africa, Gandhi returned to India where he continued his struggle, although this time against British rule. His approach, which involved non-cooperation, non-violence and peaceful resistance, was typically met by the heavy hand of the British Army. But it wasn't until the Amritsar massacre in 1919 – when the Army opened fire on a peaceful protest of unarmed men, women and children – that the tide turned. Gandhi continued to press home the rights of his fellow Indians for almost another thirty years. After nearly a lifetime of struggle against oppression, he finally witnessed his dream come true when India gained independence from Britain on 15 August 1947. However, he was killed by a fellow Indian at a prayer meeting just a few months later, in January 1948.

Many of us may feel trapped by the need to conform and yearn to escape the chains, but the majority of us do nothing about it. There are plenty of reasons for this, not least the fear of personal risk. But that pales into insignificance when you consider what Gandhi had to endure.

HERE'S AN IDEA FOR YOU...

Consider what conforming means to you. Are you crushed by it? If so, think what areas of your life you could change to allow your true self and personality to come through. Maybe it's through your hobbies or a particular sport or, if you are especially brave, through your work.

20 NOTHING IS AT LAST SACRED BUT THE INTEGRITY OF YOUR OWN MIND

Acting with integrity sets you aside from the majority, but can you step up to the plate?

Emerson believed that in the final analysis the integrity of your own mind was the most important thing you needed in order to be self-reliant. By maintaining your integrity you could avoid many of the pitfalls in life caused by a lack of it and, more importantly, prevent people who might want to control you – those in power, your employer and institutions such as the church – from having an undue influence over you.

DEFINING IDEA...

You are already of consequence in the world if you are known as a man of strict integrity.
– GRENVILLE KLEISER, AUTHOR

Integrity, which is the consistency of actions, principles, expectations and outcomes, is a quality that is both rare and difficult to maintain, and one that appears to be missing in many walks of life. It is a sad fact that few people seem able to maintain a true sense of integrity and although many talk a good game, the majority are found wanting. Is it too much to ask that each and every one of us acts with integrity? Probably not, and yet when we look at the behaviour of people, and especially those in the public eye, they disappoint us. They espouse virtues that we should all adhere to, but they fail to adhere to them themselves.

The fact of the matter is that there are very few people, organisations or indeed institutions which demonstrate true integrity. We have politicians complaining that they are being unfairly treated after having been discovered making 'creative' use of their expenses. We see organisations exploiting their workforces in order to grossly overpay their CEOs and we see bankers back at the trough, despite having brought the financial system to the brink of collapse. The key point to all this is that once there is incongruence between words and actions, trust is irrevocably broken and rebuilding it can take a considerable amount of time. What is very encouraging, though, is that there is change in the air. We are already witnessing a shift as the old guard, or those who have long outstayed their welcome, are being cast aside to give those with fresh ideas and greater integrity a chance to make a difference. We have seen it in the United States where Barack Obama is stepping up to the challenges of a nation in crisis and a broken healthcare system; we have seen it in Japan where the near-institutionalised regime which existed since the end of World War II has been swept aside in favour of an inexperienced opposition – and I am sure we will see it in many other countries too.

Ultimately, acting with integrity requires honesty in your words and consistency in your actions. People trust those who are direct in expressing their views and predictable in acting within a known set of principles. Inconsistency suggests that leaders are dishonest or self-serving and as a result they are rarely, if ever, trusted. Thank heavens the world is finally waking up to the fact.

HERE'S AN IDEA FOR YOU...

Sit down with a sheet of paper and write down what integrity means to you. Consider what levels of integrity you expect from your leaders, your work colleagues, and your friends and family. Do they meet your expectations? And what about yourself?

21 HOW EASILY WE CAPITULATE TO BADGES AND NAMES...

It's amazing to think just how easily people can be influenced by a brand.

Emerson was unimpressed at the way people were easily swayed by 'large societies and dead institutions'. He believed that they had far too much influence over the general public and, I assume, felt that they made it harder for individuals to both form and then maintain their own beliefs and opinions. Perhaps Emerson was a bit of an oddity in that he was a free thinker in a time when the availability of up-to-date information was still quite limited. Most people would have had little choice but to rely on the institutions of the day to provide them with a sense of what was going on. This would have come with some risks as people can be easily influenced without access to a range of ideas, opinions and information.

DEFINING IDEA...

The power of the brand name to consumers is a shortcut – it provides a way to simplify things.
– KEVIN KELLER, WIRED MAGAZINE

In many ways we are no different today. Perhaps the church has less sway over us these days and it is clear that political parties have virtually no influence at all, but this doesn't mean that we are any more forthright in expressing and maintaining our own opinions than people were back in the 1840s. Sadly, we capitulate just as readily, although today it is more likely to be to big brands than dead institutions, despite the huge amount of information that we can access at our finger tips via the Internet.

Brands and the companies behind them exert a huge influence over our opinions. It is well known that brands provide an important shortcut to our buying decisions and billions are pumped into developing and reinforcing brands every year (for good reason – they boost sales). The reason why we may love Coke, shop at Tesco or eat at McDonald's is in part because they are able to influence us through advertising. But brands can do more than just make us buy products; they can also affect our opinions. For example, many corporations are waking up to the power they have over our views and opinions and are using their brands to influence us, though sometimes in a positive way. Take Starbucks. It has done much to increase our awareness of Fairtrade coffee, for instance, and has been promoting green issues such as reduction in waste and increasing recycling.

Maybe we have a reverse problem to the one which Emerson saw. In the absence of readily available information people will look to institutions and other bodies to fill the void, and where we have too much we will seek shortcuts to make it easy for us to arrive at an opinion. With so much information available to us and so little time to sift through it all, we just don't know where to start. So it should come as no surprise that we are just as easily swayed today as we were in the past.

HERE'S AN IDEA FOR YOU...

How influenced are you by big brands? Write down a list of brands you can recall without prompting and determine how they influence you – is it just on purchases, or is there more to it? If you think you are overly influenced, consider how you could reduce the effect.

22 THERE IS THE MAN AND HIS VIRTUES

Big displays of charity often mask an ulterior motive.

Emerson made an important distinction between an individual and their virtues and was in agreement with the popular view of the time that virtues were the exception rather than the rule. He believed that most people who completed a good deed or made a charitable gesture were doing so as some kind of penance and were not doing it out of any genuine desire. He stated that 'Men do what is called a good action, as some piece of courage or charity, much as they would pay a fine in expiation of daily non-appearance on parade. Their works are done as an apology or extenuation of their living in the world as invalids and the insane pay a high board. Their virtues are penances.'

Perhaps he was being a bit harsh, but he certainly had a point. Doing good deeds and completing a charitable act is something that has to be heartfelt and not something that you do because you want to make a big show of it.

DEFINING IDEA...
It is a kingly act to assist the fallen.
– MOTHER TERESA

Although getting involved with a charitable event, or indeed the very act of giving to a charity, is something that many millions of people do across the world, there does seem to be too much of a song and dance made about it by those with money and status, and (of course) by celebrities. We see the famous, wealthy and well-heeled rubbing shoulders at major charity events which are heavily publicised and incredibly expensive to organise. You do have to wonder whether they are there because they truly believe in what the charity is doing or just because they want to be in the public eye (again). In most cases they have probably been told to attend by an agent or public relations department. Cynical, perhaps – but many celebrities who 'support' charities give very little to charity themselves and most expect a payment in return for turning up. Yes, charities have to promote the issues they are trying to address as it is a very crowded market out there, but a lot of these events make very little money once all the costs have been totted up.

Our role model for charity shouldn't be a big event or a few celebrities who have suddenly found that they care about something more important than themselves. It should be someone like Mother Teresa who started her work with the poor of Calcutta in 1946. In the early days she had to beg for food and supplies and although she experienced doubt and loneliness, she continued to support the homeless, crippled, hungry and unwanted of the world. When she died in 1997 she had had dedicated forty-five years of her life to the poor and dying and the mission she founded was operating in 123 locations around the world. Not once did she make a big show about it; she just got on with it instead.

HERE'S AN IDEA FOR YOU...

If you are going to do something for charity, go about it in a low-key way. Think about what really matters to you and choose to support a charity that is in alignment with your beliefs. Don't do the charity thing because you feel you have to, or for tax breaks; do it because you want to.

23 MY LIFE IS FOR ITSELF AND NOT FOR SPECTACLE

Many people want to live their life in the public eye, but the burden is often too much to bear.

DEFINING IDEA...

Your life changes. Everything has to be done perfectly, and I didn't follow that.

~ SHANNEN DOHERTY, ACTRESS

If Emerson were alive today I am sure he would have a field day commenting on society, and I am certain he would have a lot to say about reality TV. As someone who believed that your life was for yourself and not for show, he would probably dismiss it out of hand, along with those who wanted to star in such programmes. He did, of course, live before the invention of the television and long before Andy Warhol came up with the now infamous 'fifteen minutes of fame' statement, but even back then he could see the virtue of living a normal life outside of the public eye. Indeed, he felt that a life should be genuine and steady rather than glittering and unsteady. And I agree. I'm no fan of reality television, in which generally unappealing people vie for fame and fortune by dating a would-be suitor, dancing, singing, cooking, performing humiliating acts in jungles or living in a house isolated from the outside world for weeks at a time – all on air and in front of millions of viewers. As the contestants jockey for the attention of either the disinterested judges who pour scorn on their limited talents or the viewers who can vote them off, they show up some of the worst aspects of human nature. They should really stick to living a normal life: going to work every day, shopping on a Saturday, looking after the kids and so on. Such an ordinary existence is now almost considered second best.

What many fail to understand is that celebrities are wired differently from the rest of us. As well as being incredibly vain and narcissistic, they crave attention, are over-confident in their abilities, lack empathy and behave erratically. And the fewer real skills they have, the more desperate they are to hang onto the celebrity lifestyle. There is also a massive downside to being a celebrity which many who seek it fail to understand until it's too late: their life really is a spectacle, played out for all to see – warts and all. Their lives are lived on television and in trashy magazines and newspapers, watched and read by 'normal' people who are desperate to hear about the latest twists and turns of their favourite celebs' lives. But how many times do we see pictures of celebs falling out of nightclubs at 3 in the morning, or checking into the Priory for their latest drink or drug problem? The burden of being filmed every waking hour or being chased down the street by the paparazzi is often too much to bear. The reason why so many celebrities crash and burn is that they can't cope with being perpetually in the public eye; there is no down time. Many complain, but they can't have it both ways, and nor should they.

HERE'S AN IDEA FOR YOU...

Relish what really matters in your life; the simple things like your friends and family, your hobbies and perhaps your work. Enjoy the freedoms you have and recognise the value of living a normal life outside of the public eye.

24 FEW AND MEAN AS MY GIFTS MAY BE

If only we would accept our gifts we would all be a lot happier (and even talented).

Emerson's brand of self-help was not focused on people trying to be something they were not, which is what we are typically fed by the self-help movement these days. Instead, he was of the firm belief that you should accept the gifts that you had been born with.

This makes a lot of sense, as much discontent is caused by wanting to be something that you could never be. You might want to be a top-notch tennis player like Rafael Nadal, or perhaps an amazing composer like Mozart, but being that requires two things. First, you have to possess some modicum of latent capability; second, you have to display huge amounts of dedication to reach the top of your game. Many people might be OK on the first point, but 99.99% of them are unable (because of other commitments) or unwilling (because it is bloody hard work) to put the hours in to be as successful as Nadal or Mozart. Indeed, if only to confirm the fact, a study into what separated talented musicians who went on to become virtuosos from those who ended up as music teachers was nothing more than practice. The musicians in the study were equally competent, but those who succeeded were the ones who put in the most practice. This shouldn't surprise us. We should recognise that great sports stars, businesspeople, academics and so on sacrifice a great deal to be the best they can. In many respects they have been lucky enough to spot their talent and do something about it.

One way to view your gifts is through the lens of a search for meaning. We all crave some kind of importance to our lives, as it is this which spurs us on and gives us our sense of purpose. Highly talented people like Nadal are fortunate enough to have found it early on in their lives (or it was recognised and honed from a young age by their parents), but most of us are not that lucky. The good news is that we are all capable of finding meaning in our lives and as a result uncovering our true talents – not those required by our parents or workplace.

One man who has helped to show how is Victor Frankl. You may not have heard of him, but he is someone who managed to unravel what it is to find meaning and he did it in some of the most terrible places imaginable – Dachau, Auschwitz and other concentration camps. Frankl spent three years in captivity and was one of the few survivors. He survived because he found meaning in the hellish environment of the camps, and his survival depended on understanding what the environment expected of him and not the other way round. He went on to develop Logotherapy, a branch of psychotherapy which has helped millions of people find meaning in their lives.

HERE'S AN IDEA FOR YOU...

What does your environment (work, home, family, etc.) expect of you? Is there a match? Rather than try to mould the world around you, try to see what it needs from you. You may find, for example, that you're in a job which doesn't allow your true talents to shine. What could you change so that they do?

25 WHAT I MUST DO IS ALL THAT CONCERNS ME, NOT WHAT PEOPLE THINK

When you know something is right, you are better off not listening to the advice everyone wants to give you.

DEFINING IDEA...

Wise men don't need advice. Fools won't take it.

– BENJAMIN FRANKLIN

Emerson believed that one of the toughest challenges we faced was the ability to do something when everyone else around us was telling us to do something else or, worse still, offering their opinions as to the efficacy of our actions. He believed 'it was easy in the world to live after the world's opinion and by the same token easy in solitude to live after your own.' However, 'the great man is he who, in the midst of the crowd, keeps with perfect sweetness the independence of solitude'.

It is true that whenever you are going to undertake anything significant in life, there are always plenty of people who will give you the benefit of their advice. The key thing to remember about advice is that you have to ask for it first. Unfortunately, that doesn't stop people from giving it, even though most of it is not based upon first-hand experience. Holding your own whilst everyone tells you that what you're about to do is crazy or wrong, and wants to inform you of a better way of achieving it, is quite difficult. I remember when I was 17 and decided that I wanted to pursue a surveying degree. I did my research, chose carefully and selected the university I wanted to attend. Then the advice started. My physics teacher told me that I should have chosen civil engineering because her husband did it. Then my head of year had a crack; this time telling me surveying was academically below me. Even the headmaster had tried to convince me to change my mind, even bringing in a civil engineer to tell me I was making a big mistake. I stuck to my guns and really enjoyed the course.

If you have ever watched Dragons' Den, the television series in which budding entrepreneurs put their ideas to a bunch of po-faced tycoons, you'll understand Emerson's viewpoint. As the entrepreneurs make their pitch they are offered advice about how good or how bad their idea is (mostly bad, it seems). If the tycoons believe it's a good idea, they will aim to secure as large a share of the company as possible for a few thousand pounds and the occasional day's support. I can never understand why the budding business big-shots would be willing to give so much of their idea away, but that's another story. Most of the entrepreneurs are torn apart and belittled by the tycoons and told that their ideas are rubbish with no chance of success. And although many walk away crushed by the experience, you get the odd one or two who are spurred on by the rejection and 'advice' and make a huge success of their business idea. Listening to what other people might think isn't always the best strategy. For the most part, you should follow your instincts.

HERE'S AN IDEA FOR YOU...

The next time you have to do something important or take a critical decision, don't let the amateur advice-givers try and tell you what you should or shouldn't do. Stick to your guns. If you do need advice, make sure you get it from someone who has the experience and ability to give you a balanced opinion.

26 IF I KNOW YOUR SECT, I ANTICIPATE YOUR ARGUMENT

'Groupthink' suppresses original thinking, which can be highly dangerous.

Emerson was of the opinion that if he knew what beliefs you espoused, he would know what your opinions were. From simple observation we can see this is true: after all, look at any member of any political party and you can probably guess what they will say before they even open their mouth. This kind of behaviour is true of any tightly knit group.

DEFINING IDEA...

A camel is a horse designed by committee.

~ SIR ALEC ISSIGONIS, DESIGNER OF THE MINI

Although it might be nice to know where you stand, there is a fundamental problem associated with groupthink. Groupthink is all about maintaining the status quo and avoiding conflict within the group. This typically means that the consensus goes unchallenged as group members are reluctant to raise issues, concerns, ideas or opinions which could disrupt the group's dynamics or which could introduce conflict. This may lead to hasty or irrational decisions, especially when people are averse to airing their concerns for fear of upsetting other members of the group.

One example of groupthink on a massive scale has to do with the credit crunch. Although we might all think that it was the bankers who screwed up so royally, it was – according to a number of commentators – the MBA graduates who were behind it. The MBA, which is designed to educate people in the art and science of business, has taken a bit of a beating since the collapse of the financial system in 2007; mainly, it has to be said, because many of the people associated with causing the crisis held one.

It's now commonly believed that MBA programmes tended to attract greedy young executives with little or no real business understanding or experience. And, once in the programmes, said executives were fed management theories and business concepts which for the most part were ill thought out. The executives who attended these programmes were taught identical concepts and ended up thinking in the same way. As a result, they not only came out of business school spouting the same incomprehensible jargon but were also incapable of original thought. And armed with an MBA they also believed themselves to be Masters of the Universe and displayed a level of arrogance that few can surpass. We shouldn't forget that almost the only place where they could earn enough money to pay off their tuition fees was investment banking. The rest, as they say, is history. No wonder that many are calling for the MBA to be overhauled.

This is perhaps a somewhat simplistic view but it does illustrate the danger of executives who have followed the same kind of educational path. Without variety and the acceptance of different opinions and viewpoints, they end up thinking the same. Although we may be members of identical institutions, or follow common educational paths, it is critical that we seek out alternative views to test the validity of those we already hold. This can help us avoid some of the pitfalls of going with the flow.

HERE'S AN IDEA FOR YOU...

The next time you are in a group watch out for the tell-tale signs of groupthink, such as no one challenging ideas being put forward, or concerns being brushed aside. If you see this happening, be willing to raise your concerns even if it does lead to a bit of conflict. The outcome will be better.

27 THIS CONFORMITY MAKES THEM FALSE

Conforming to social and organisational norms of behaviour makes sense, but sometimes we need to know when conforming is absolutely the wrong thing to do.

DEFINING IDEA...

The reward for conformity is that everyone likes you but yourself.

– RITA MAE BROWN, AUTHOR

Emerson was not a huge fan of conformity, although I am sure most of his displeasure was directed at what he considered to be the dead institutions of his time. We should recognise that, in a general sense, conformity is part and parcel of living in a functioning society; without it there would be anarchy. The same is true of organisations, as without employees conforming to the norms of behaviour, businesses would undoubtedly fail. So conformity can be good… however, Emerson did have a point when it came to misplaced conformity, as adhering to norms which are wrong or outmoded can have potentially catastrophic consequences. One appalling example is the way in which German conformity with the racial stereotypes promoted by the Nazis led to genocide. We have also seen how conforming to the norms in some poorly and even corruptly run organisations has resulted in massive losses and the collapse of major businesses. Think of Enron, Lehman Brothers, Northern Rock and the Royal Bank of Scotland. In such companies, the degree of conformity was arguably so great that no one dared to question the dubious business practices that were endemic within them; those who did were usually sacked. What is worrying is that it's bound to happen again.

A little while ago I was talking with a colleague of mine who is Malaysian and who regularly travels from his current home in Houston back to Malaysia.

When he returns to Malaysia he usually passes through Singapore, and told me about the differences between the two countries. One such difference sums up the nature of conformity very well – how people boarded buses. In Singapore, everyone lined up in an orderly queue and waited patiently until it was their turn to get on. No one made a fuss and everyone was polite. In Malaysia it was a different experience. There was no queue and it was essentially a free for all, with people literally elbowing others out of the way so they could get on first. In both cases, of course, everyone conformed to the acceptable norms of behaviour.

I am particularly fascinated by Singapore, because as a nation it is highly regimented and people are willing to give up some of their civil liberties in return for living in a very clean and safe environment. Apparently the police are all under cover so you don't know, as you are about to jay-walk across the road, if the person standing next to you is a copper. Because you don't, you're unwilling to take the risk. Everyone conforms. An extreme example, perhaps, as of course is Nazi Germany, but it does illustrate the power of conformity. Understanding that blind conformance can be dangerous is important, and you should always attempt to question whether your conformance reflects your personal beliefs or those of others.

HERE'S AN IDEA FOR YOU...

Imagine a situation at work in which conforming to the norms of behaviour would be wrong. What would you do? Raise the danger flag or toe the line? It's an interesting dilemma and one which we all face from time to time, so thinking through what you might do in such a situation is a useful exercise.

28 THE FOOLISH FACE OF PRAISE

If we were more interested in other people, perhaps they would be more interested in us.

According to Emerson, there could be nothing worse than the foolish face of praise. He gave only one illustration and that was to do with the cursory acknowledgement you might get in a conversation with another person who isn't that interested in either you or your opinion.

I'm certain that Emerson really meant acknowledgement rather than praise, and I'm sure that you have been in similar situations; I know I have. They typically happen at conferences where you are thrown together with lots of other people and feel that you have to strike up a conversation, usually over the coffee break or lunch. Most encounters are difficult and quite frankly embarrassing because although you try to get the discussion going, the other person is only interested in trying to catch the eye of someone else. Fine, you get a cursory nod here and there and a slight smile (which is more like a grimace), but you just know that they are about as interested in you as you are in them. Most people can't wait to get back into the lecture theatre.

One of the lessons which neuro-linguistic programming teaches us is that in order for us to be interesting to someone else, we have to be interested in them too. This is the basis of rapport which recognises that any relationship, no matter how fleeting, is always going to be a two-way street. And because we never quite know how someone is going to respond, we have to be ready to adjust our response to any given situation. Two of the most effective ways of building rapport are mirroring and mixing up your language.

Mirroring is about aligning your behaviour patterns to those of the person you are communicating with so that you create congruence. You can mirror the other person's body movements, the tonal quality of their voice, their attitudes and even their breathing. To do so means reflecting back to the other person a pattern of behaviour that is most like their own. It's about more than just copying and if you make it too obvious they will probably just think you are a bit weird and walk off. The key is to be subtle.

The other thing you can do is to use language the other person can tune into – which you can discover very quickly by listening to the words they use. There are three types: visual (words like see and show), auditory (words like sound and hear), and kinaesthetic (words like feel and structure). If you want to build rapport rapidly you should use similar words, whether they are visual, auditory or kinaesthetic.

Taken together, mirroring and the careful use of language allow you to make the other person feel comfortable in your company, more likely to engage with you and even to agree with you. Roll on the next conference!

HERE'S AN IDEA FOR YOU...

Practise your matching and mirroring skills on those around you. Do it with people you know, such as your partner or children (generally a safe place to start). As you practise, see if you can begin to lead their behaviour and see if they start to mirror you.

29 FOR NONCONFORMITY THE WORLD WHIPS YOU WITH ITS DISPLEASURE

Being different from other people is usually frowned upon, but you shouldn't take this too seriously as the disapproval is rarely heartfelt.

DEFINING IDEA...

Conformity is the jailer of freedom and the enemy of growth.

~ JOHN F. KENNEDY

Emerson spends a lot of time on the topic of conformity, and it is clear that he wasn't a fan of it at all. However, when you think about it, we are all conformists in one way or another. We conform to the expectations of our employers when at work and we usually conform to the rules (both written and unwritten) of society when going about our daily lives. There is a simple reason for this and that's about fitting in and being accepted and, as a result, being perceived to be a 'normal' person. It's probably fair to say that most people want to have a relatively quiet life. As long as there are sufficient degrees of freedom which allow them to do broadly what they want to, then they are happy to conform. By the same token, people are happy to follow the rules within the workplace as long as they are suitably rewarded and looked after. From this perspective, at least, conforming seems to makes sense, doesn't it?

There is, of course, another and possibly more important reason why we tend to conform and that's to avoid the short shrift that awaits those who choose not to do so. Whether inside or outside of work, people who don't conform are typically pilloried and considered strange or even abnormal; the majority of us are wary of them. In extreme cases they are considered outcasts and are treated as such (rather like lepers who may live in colonies, which bizarrely still exist in certain parts of the world).

Emerson saw more danger in conformity than nonconformity. He believed that conformance prevented people from trusting their own judgement and, as a result, being less likely to pursue their dreams and seize opportunities when they presented themselves. In other words, being unwilling to stick their neck out for fear of being laughed at and ridiculed. He also noted that people's opinions about what was considered to be right or wrong behaviour were largely governed by what they read in the newspapers. As a result they were apt to change their opinions frequently – and if that's the case, why bother considering them? If you think about it, it's the same today; we see it all the time in the way that we are told, via the media, what is good for us and what's bad, how we ought to behave and so on. Emerson's advice was simple: all we need to do is to be able to estimate a sour face and look beyond the displeasure displayed on it. It is clear that some people's opinions are worth listening to, but in the most part they have to be taken with a pinch of salt. And if you are going to realise your true potential, you sometimes have to ignore the court of public opinion.

HERE'S AN IDEA FOR YOU...

How do you cope with feedback? Do you take it to heart or do you let it wash over you? Are you someone who would prefer to conform to avoid criticism? If so, consider how it undermines your confidence and commit to listening to your heart rather than other people.

30 THE POWER OF THE MOB

The educated know how to control their anger, but mobs don't and that's when things can get nasty.

DEFINING IDEA...

The mob has many heads,
but no brains.

– THOMAS FULLER, SEVENTEENTH-CENTURY
BRITISH CLERGYMAN AND WRITER

Emerson understood that there was a fundamental difference in how people expressed their anger in society. Those at the top – the educated elite, if you like – were able to express their feelings in an erudite way, could put their points across clearly and were often well connected. They were, typically, heard because they were restrained and managed to hold their animal feelings in check. Those at the bottom of society, who were normally poorly educated, had no such ability and instead tended towards demonstrations and violence. This was almost the only way in which they could be heard and even though many demonstrations ended up in bloodshed and failed to make any difference whatsoever, there were occasions when the mob forced a change in society. For example, the mob that stormed the Bastille in 1789 heralded huge social change in France (even though this did involve the Terror, in which thousands were guillotined). In a similar way, the mob that executed the Boston Tea Party in 1773 set in train the turn of events that led to the War of Independence and gave birth to the United States.

Even today, when the world is arguably more democratic than it has ever been, many people feel so disenfranchised that they think they have to take to the streets. It's a shame that a large body of people feel that they are not listened to and that those in power are not concerned about the things that matter to the average person, even in Western democracies. Most feel that the only way to make governments sit up and listen is to protest. And, as in the past, some are more successful at stimulating change than others. The demonstrations and riots that occur every time the G20 meets rarely have an impact, but what we've been seeing in Iran might eventually succeed. As usual, though, the heavy hand of the state is there to quell any uprising. It is worth recalling the words of Edmund Burke, the great Tory philosopher, who said in 1796, 'If the people are turbulent and riotous, nothing is to be done for them on account of their evil dispositions. If they are obedient and loyal, nothing is to be done for them, because their being quiet and contented is proof that they feel no grievance'. In other words, those at the bottom lose out either way.

The method by which the UK's 2006 fuel strike was managed provides a good example of how non-violent protesting can lead to change, even if it's only temporary. The protestors forced the Chancellor to delay the proposed fuel tax increase after blockading refineries and gaining public support. They coordinated their actions through mobile phones and the Internet which proved difficult to disrupt, making it very easy for them to remain in control. This shows how technology has improved the likelihood of people being heard, which has to be a good thing.

HERE'S AN IDEA FOR YOU...

What is your opinion on demonstrations? How would you deal with something that made you angry? Think about it carefully. Are you someone who would take to the streets or seek to find a way to lobby those in power by alternative means?

31 BUT WHY SHOULD YOU KEEP YOUR HEAD OVER YOUR SHOULDER?

Too many of us worry about what other people might think, but seeking out and giving feedback is an essential ingredient of success.

Emerson lived during relatively stable times, so when he wrote Self-Reliance in 1841 the type of fear that he was principally concerned about was the fear of what other people might think of you, especially if you appeared to be inconsistent in your opinion or actions. He felt this was irrational and something that undermined our ability to trust ourselves, which he believed was a critical foundation of self-reliance. He reckoned that people spent too much time looking over their shoulders and worrying about what others felt about them. He was probably right, although things have changed a lot since then.

DEFINING IDEA...

The mediocre teacher tells. The good teacher explains. The superior teacher demonstrates. The great teacher inspires.
– WILLIAM ARTHUR WARD, AMERICAN SCHOLAR

Although worrying about what other people might think about you is often an unnecessary waste of time and energy – especially if it is baseless and not followed up by actually asking – soliciting feedback is essential these days. We live in a world where the giving and receiving of feedback is easier than ever: look at any website and there's an opportunity to provide feedback, for instance. The same is true of restaurants and of course the workplace (I'll come back to that in a moment). Asking your customers and clients about your service and how you can improve it is probably one of the best things you can do. The more enlightened organisations are taking the feedback thing even further by asking customers to engage with them on product development and innovation.

If it works for organisations, it can surely work for you. None of us are islands and although being self-reliant is as important as it has ever been, there is always room for improvement. Therefore you can, and indeed should, ask for feedback from those around you. You can choose the people you seek feedback from, of course, and determine what kind you want. For example, you could find someone who can coach you in certain aspects of your professional and personal life, and there is no harm in having a mentor who is able to help test out your ideas and review your aspirations. The key thing is to approach feedback in a way that is constructive and additive. In other words, you need to be in control of it. And don't forget the Internet, as this is often a superb way to seek feedback from experts and most are more than happy to give you a quick opinion.

In case you needed to be reminded why feedback is so important, you should remember that the lack of performance coaching and feedback is one of the biggest sources of employee disengagement and turnover – so you ignore the giving of feedback at your peril. Of course, you do have to remember that giving feedback is not about picking up on all someone's bad points or focusing on something at which they are not necessarily skilled. That's no use at all.

HERE'S AN IDEA FOR YOU...

Are there areas of your life where you think you could benefit from a bit of feedback, coaching or mentoring? Note them down and find yourself a coach. Remember to be willing to receive feedback positively, as this makes it much more effective.

32 WITH CONSISTENCY A GREAT SOUL HAS SIMPLY NOTHING TO DO

A closed mind is fatal; it makes your world shrink.

DEFINING IDEA...

Anyone who stops learning is old, whether at twenty or eighty.

– HENRY FORD

Although being inconsistent is often perceived to be a bad thing, Emerson felt that foolish consistency was far worse. He was referring to maintaining a point of view or opinion that was patently wrong, despite evidence pointing to the contrary. He called such foolish consistency 'the hobgoblin of little minds'. Such small-mindedness is usually the product of a closed mind and typified by someone who is uninterested in learning. It might have been acceptable 150 years ago, but in today's knowledge economy, where learning continues to take centre stage, having a closed mind can have a huge impact on earning power. Keeping an open mind requires that we master how we learn, and the best way we can do this is to follow the four steps.

When we learn anything, we typically pass through four distinct phases. Phase 1, unconscious incompetence, is where we don't know that we don't know. We have yet to learn about a subject, such as driving a car or riding a bike. The next phase is conscious incompetence. As we begin to learn something, we are acutely aware of our failings and inability to master the skill we are trying to learn. Next comes conscious competence, where we have begun to master the skill but still have to maintain our concentration and are prone to errors; it is thought that we learn most during this stage. The final phase is unconscious competence, where we apply the newly learned skill automatically. When we have reached this stage the unconscious mind takes control, leaving the conscious mind to think about other things; now the skill has been hard-wired into the brain.

The four stages model is useful for three reasons. First, it provides a clear illustration of how we move from knowing little about a new subject to mastering it. Second, it manages our expectations during the learning process by guiding us through the steps we have to go through. Finally, it suggests that there are some inherent dangers in being unconsciously competent, especially when we come to rely too much on our tacit knowledge.

This last point is important because operating at the unconsciously competent level can result in developing bad habits and failing to change as the environment alters. It is sometimes necessary, therefore, to unlearn what we already know and then relearn it, taking into account the changes around us. Because it can be very difficult for us to see the need to change, it is beneficial to seek feedback from peers (or a personal coach) to help identify where change and the necessary relearning is required. Learning to learn is probably one of the best things you can do to avoid ever having a closed mind – and it can be a lot of fun, too.

HERE'S AN IDEA FOR YOU...

Think about your approach to learning. Are you someone who is content to rely on the knowledge they already have, or do you seek out new information to update and change what you already know? Why not take an aspect of your work and determine whether or not it could benefit from a bit of a knowledge update?

33 IS IT SO BAD, THEN, TO BE MISUNDERSTOOD?

We should value those in society who are willing to challenge orthodoxy; they make us think.

As you read Self-Reliance, you get the feeling that Emerson wasn't a great fan of the norms of behaviour in nineteenth-century America. He certainly wasn't one to mince his words and I wonder how his views went down with his fellow Americans… however, he made plenty of valid points, so I hope at least some of them were listening. One of the key points (at least for me) was his view on being misunderstood. Rather than being something to be concerned about, he believed it was great to be misunderstood because it meant that you were willing to challenge the received wisdom of the day.

DEFINING IDEA...

Be not disturbed at being misunderstood; be disturbed rather at not being understanding.
– CHINESE PROVERB

In this respect, his heroes were people like Aristotle, Newton, Galileo, Socrates and Martin Luther and 'every wise and pure spirit that ever took flesh'. Without such people, we might still be living in the Dark Ages, or at the very least it would have taken a lot longer to truly understand the world around us. And I tend to agree with Emerson that these people were the heroes of their day. Standing up to the church in Galileo's time was a very bold move; society and thinking were closed to new ideas and anything which challenged the orthodoxy of the church was dismissed out of hand. It was a society that shunned insight and learning.

Fortunately things are better now, although there are plenty of people who refuse to allow new thinking and knowledge to alter their opinions. For example, even today, when the evidence appears to support Darwin's theory of evolution, there are those in society who believe in Intelligent Design – the notion that God designed all the flora and fauna of the world to evolve over time. In other words, evolution does not happen in response to the changing surroundings, but was planned from the start. I wonder, therefore, if God designed the human race to pollute the world so much that some species have to evolve as a result? In some American schools Intelligent Design is being taught instead of Darwinism, which has been summarily discarded. Ideally, both ideas should be discussed side by side so that the students can weigh them up and decide which one they want to believe in. Rejecting knowledge out of hand like this takes us back, not on.

We should all be more willing to embrace the forward thinkers of our time because they provide us with the foil with which we can develop a more rounded and better understanding of the world around us. As a result, we should be aiming to use new information about a subject to test our current understanding. And rather than rejecting it because it doesn't fit our world view, we should see how it improves it – even if it does mean discarding some firmly held beliefs.

HERE'S AN IDEA FOR YOU...

When you read or hear about something that is counter to your own world view or understanding, what do you do? Do you dismiss it and maintain your view, or does it make you think that you may need to update your knowledge? The latter approach is far more useful as it helps to build a flexible and open mind.

34 THE CONSISTENCY OF CHARACTER

Who do you think you are?

Emerson believed that someone's true character would always shine through, no matter what they did. To some extent he was right, but it is fair to say that the majority of us do not really understand ourselves to the degree that Emerson inferred when he made the following statement: 'a character is like an acrostic or Alexandrian stanza – read it forward, backward, or across, it still spells the same thing'. Most of us drift through our lives without fully understanding what makes us tick or makes us unique. We may have a vague inkling but it is never fully explored. That's why television programmes such as *Who Do You Think You Are?* are so interesting. It's fascinating to watch celebrities find out about their roots and ancestors, as so much is unknown to them before the show; some are surprised by what they find out and many are shocked. Although our roots help to explain some of our character, there is a lot more to character than what has been handed down from our parents and grandparents.

DEFINING IDEA...

Know thyself.

~ SOCRATES

In simple terms, we comprise two selfs, the true self and the ego. Unless we are very fortunate, our ego is usually detached to a greater or lesser extent from our true self. There are many reasons for this, such as how we were brought up as a child, how we want to present ourselves to the world, and how we choose to protect ourselves from being hurt. Freud and many other well-known psychoanalysts had plenty to say about egos, but there just isn't the space to do so here. The true self, the real you, is where your character lies. This is the free spirit that often remains caged and held in check by the ego, either because it is fragile or has never had the opportunity to see the light of day. It is the artist inside an accountant or the mechanic inside a waiter. Eric Berne, who developed Transactional Analysis (the parent–adult–child thing), summed this difference up very neatly when he said 'Many a man with the chemistry of a great ballet dancer spends his time dancing with other people's dishes in a lunchroom, and others with genes of a mathematician pass their days juggling other people's papers in the back room of a bank or bookie joint. But within his chemical limitation, whatever they are, each man has enormous possibilities for determining his own fate.'

What we can say is that the greater the distance between your ego and your true self, the bigger the problems you tend to experience, especially as you grow older. As you age, the ego gradually weakens and the true self begins to emerge – the classic mid-life crisis. It is then that you realise who you really are. Some are lucky to experience this early on in their lives; others are less fortunate.

HERE'S AN IDEA FOR YOU...

How well do you know yourself? How would you define your character and do you understand why you do what you do and behave the way you do? Ask people who are close to you, such as your spouse or long-term friends. They often know your character better than you do.

RALPH WALDO EMERSON'S *SELF-RELIANCE*

35 YOUR GENUINE ACTION WILL EXPLAIN ITSELF

If you really want to see someone's true character don't listen to what they say, observe what they do.

Emerson believed that actions were the best test of an individual and that conformity meant nothing. It was easy to conform because it didn't require much in the way of originality and going with the flow was always going to be the path of least resistance. In the final analysis, it was what people did that really mattered, as actions were a much clearer reflection of someone's character than anything they said.

DEFINING IDEA...
Talk doesn't cook rice.
– CHINESE PROVERB

This makes a lot of sense, as the body of knowledge about communication shows that only 7% of a message is communicated verbally – by the words we use. Of the remaining 93% non-verbal communication, 38% comes through the tonality of the voice and 55% through facial expressions and other body-language signals. This was exceptionally well demonstrated during the 1984 United States presidential campaign. Tapes of interviews between the candidates Ronald Reagan and Walter Mondale and three news channels – CBS, NBC and ABC – were made as part of an experiment. Excerpts were taken from these tapes in which all references to the candidates were removed. These were then shown, with the sound turned off, to a group of randomly chosen people who were asked to score the expressions of the interviewer concerned. The scoring ranged from 1 (extremely negative) to 21 (extremely positive). Whereas two of the interviewers were scored much the same for both candidates, the ABC interviewer was rated much higher when talking to Reagan. The researchers concluded that this represented a significant bias toward Reagan. This initial finding was followed up to see what the impacts were on the voters themselves. The results were profound. In every case where voters had watched the ABC interview, they voted for Reagan in greater numbers than those who had watched either CBS or NBC. It appeared that the facial expressions used by the ABC presenter were enough to influence the electorate to vote for Reagan rather than Mondale (Malcolm Gladwell discusses this in more detail in The Tipping Point). The experiment was repeated in subsequent presidential campaigns with similar results.

Although we all probably like to think we are clever enough to say one thing and do another, it is easy for our bodies to give us away. Talk, as they say, is cheap and actions certainly speak louder than words. This is because our bodies are controlled by the limbic system, which is the old part of our brain. It controls our nervous system, our bodily functions and, of course, our emotions. Just imagine if you had to actually think every time you had to do anything – breathe, move a finger… It just wouldn't work. That's why it's automatic and that's why there is always congruence between how you actually feel and what your body does. You can talk all you like, but your body gives you away. Emerson was right; your genuine action will always explain itself.

HERE'S AN IDEA FOR YOU...

Become a people watcher. Take every opportunity to see if there is congruence between what people say and what their bodies tell you. A great place to start is at work or when watching politicians on television. Tune into the discrepancies between voice and body.

36 GREATNESS APPEALS TO THE FUTURE

Everyone loves you when you're dead!

Emerson was, at least to some extent, quite unique among philosophers in that he appeared to be loved and well respected whilst he was still alive. That isn't always the case, as many leaders, politicians, scientists and businessmen find out to their horror. It is fair to say, though, that history often tends to view people through a much gentler lens. Emerson believed this was because we are able to view the past without any connection to the present. In other words, there are no consequences – good or bad. As he said, 'Honor is venerable to us because it is no ephemeris. It is always ancient virtue. We worship it to-day because it is not of to-day. We love it and pay it homage, because it is not a trap for our love and homage, but is self-dependent, self-derived, and therefore of an old immaculate pedigree, even if shown in a young person.'

DEFINING IDEA...

He is one of those people who would be enormously improved by death.

~ H. H. MUNRO, AUTHOR

If you think about it there are plenty of examples which illustrate Emerson's point. Many of the world's leaders – and especially those in power before, during and after the Second World War – fall into this camp. Take Winston Churchill, who has been voted as Britain's greatest person. This was the man who sent around 500,000 French, English and Australian soldiers to Gallipoli in 1915 only for over half of them to be killed on the Turkish beaches. The disastrous and ill-thought-out campaign tarnished his reputation and yet we only really remember him for his courage and determined leadership during the Battle of Britain in 1940. Then there is Stalin, whose purges of the Soviet military in the 1930s and carving up of Poland with Germany at the start of the war were pushed to the background after his heroic leadership and defeat of the Germans following the battle of Stalingrad in 1943. Many Russians still admire him, despite knowing about his atrocities both before and after the war. Here's another example. Joan of Arc, despite leading the French against the invasion of the English during the Hundred Years' War and lifting the siege of Orléans in 1429, was sold by the Burgundians to the English and burned at the stake. Although it was her own people who handed her over, they eventually made her a saint. And, finally, it's well known that US presidents' approval ratings usually rise after they have stepped down.

Apart from suggesting that history nearly always looks back with a certain degree of amnesia and generosity, it also suggests that if you are willing to stand up for what you believe in and consistently do the right thing, history will thank you for it. It also demonstrates very powerfully that although you may need to make some tough decisions from time to time, the results are often viewed favourably once the dust has settled. History, it seems, honours the brave.

HERE'S AN IDEA FOR YOU...

How do you want to be remembered? Sit down and write down your own epitaph. It may seem a bit odd but not only will it give you an insight into what you might still want to achieve, it will also highlight those areas of your life which you could change.

37 AN INSTITUTION IS THE LENGTHENED SHADOW OF ONE MAN

Behind any great institution, any great company and any great event, there is usually one person.

One of Emerson's clearest messages in Self-Reliance is that we should all live up to our destiny. In his words, 'Every true man is a cause, a country, and an age; requires infinite spaces and numbers and time fully to accomplish his design; – and posterity seem to follow his steps as a train of clients. A man Caesar is born, and for ages after we have a Roman Empire. Christ is born, and millions of minds so grow and cleave to his genius; that he is confounded with virtue and possible of man.' From this he concluded that every institution was the 'lengthened shadow' of one individual. This is, of course, true as it is usually the founder member of an institution that we tend to remember, and who also tends to be honoured. Those who come after may be just as smart but are more likely to be forgotten.

It's a bit like the first mover advantage in business; we usually remember the first company that enters the market, not the second or third. For example, we are likely to remember that it was Tesco that brought in the first supermarket loyalty card (the Clubcard), and Toyota that launched the first hybrid car. We can recall them because they were the organisations that stepped away from the crowd and did something different or unique; they took a bold step, whilst others waited to see what happened. The same thing applies at the personal level where people are remembered for doing something that has never been done before, such as Roger Bannister running the four minute mile, Neil

Armstrong being the first man on the moon – and so on. Even though others followed in their footsteps, we have difficulty in remembering their names or achievements. It's a shame, but it doesn't mean that we shouldn't strive for greatness in everything we do.

When Emerson used the examples of Caesar and Jesus he was doing so to highlight the importance of knowing your worth, which is fundamental to realising your full potential. Many people may have dreams they want to pursue, but because they have self-doubts or listen to those around them who believe they cannot achieve them, they give up. Others have no such problem and believe in themselves so much that they are able to follow through and realise their full potential, be that in politics, business, sport or science. They have the necessary single-mindedness and self-belief to reach their goals. This is someone like the classic entrepreneur who will start a company from the back of a car, or from a market stall as Richard Branson did in the 1960s. Entrepreneurs are looked up to and venerated by their staff and, more generally, by society. And even when they have moved on or retired, they are still remembered – their business is indeed the 'lengthened shadow of one man'.

HERE'S AN IDEA FOR YOU...

Striving to do your best in everything you do is a laudable goal; you should always aim for it. Think about the main areas of your life – home, work, family, hobbies – and set yourself some personal goals in each dimension.

38 WE DENOTE THIS PRIMARY WISDOM AS INTUITION

Feeding your mind is one of the best things you can do in order to become self-reliant.

When Emerson attempts to get to the nub of why some people are more self-reliant and able to trust in their own abilities than others, he clearly finds it difficult, but he does say this: 'The inquiry leads us to that source, at once the essence of genius, of virtue, and of life, which we call Spontaneity or Instinct.' He goes on to say, 'We denote this primary wisdom as Intuition, whilst all later teachings are tuitions.' So although he finds it difficult, he suggests that instinct and wisdom have something to do with it.

DEFINING IDEA...

There comes a time when the mind takes a higher plane of knowledge but can never prove how it got there.
~ ALBERT EINSTEIN

If you unwrap this a little further, you discover that there's a strong link between knowledge and self-reliance. Having an in-depth understanding of a subject or of the world around you gives you the confidence to speak your mind, because when you are certain of something and feel that you have the facts to back up your argument, you are more likely to give your opinion. The other thing it highlights is how people with a lot of knowledge are often considered to have sound intuition. You have to question where this intuition comes from, as it didn't just happen by magic. It had to be fed by something, and that something was knowledge. A simple example of this would be a doctor who has spent years developing an understanding of cancer. With the expertise and experience gained over many years, the doctor intuitively knows the combination of signs to look for which may suggest a patient has the disease. The good thing about their 'intuition' is that they will be able to pick up a combination of signs which on their own may not signify anything, but when taken together suggests there could be a problem. They are in essence, unconsciously competent: they can operate in their specialist area without thinking about it and that's why it can come across as intuition. Doctors are but one example, and there are plenty of others you could think of. Sometimes you may even catch yourself saying something and then thinking 'how on earth did I know that?'

Although you might think that it takes a long time to build enough of an understanding of a subject to appear very knowledgeable, the surprising thing is actually how quickly you can achieve it – as long as you turn your mind to it. I've noticed that most people are quite lazy and are rarely that interested in feeding their mind any further once they have finished their formal schooling. That's where those who do go on gain their advantage. All you need is to get into the habit of learning and hoovering up knowledge. And, given that most of us look up to those who have mastered something we haven't, it won't be long before you can see that it's possible to develop a virtuous circle, one with knowledge at its core.

HERE'S AN IDEA FOR YOU...

Assess what you read and determine what changes you could make in your reading habits to increase your overall knowledge. You don't have to read encyclopaedias all the time, but magazines like New Scientist and The Economist are good places to start.

39 THOUGHTLESS PEOPLE

Being thoughtless is not just annoying, it can also be fatal.

Emerson believed that thoughtless people were too ready to contradict themselves and unable to distinguish between perception and notion. As a man who was clearly thoughtful, you could see why this annoyed him so much. He had a more important point to make, though, as the thoughtless in the world are pretty good at undermining self-reliance. Thoughtlessness comes in many different guises; it might be the flippant comment made without thinking or doing a task without fully concentrating on it. At its basic level, it's annoying because it shows that there's a lack of attention, either to the person or activity concerned. In some circumstances, however, thoughtless behaviour can be fatal.

DEFINING IDEA...

I much prefer the sharpest criticism of a single intelligent man to the thoughtless approval of the masses.

– JOHANN KEPLER

One example is the UK oil industry's terrible disaster of 6 July 1988, on the Piper Alpha North Sea oil and gas platform. It resulted in 167 deaths and was caused by the leakage of gas condensate that had built up beneath the platform and which then ignited, causing a massive explosion. The explosion started secondary oil fires, melting the riser of an upstream gas pipeline. The released gas caused a second and much larger explosion which engulfed the entire platform. The original leak of condensate occurred when members of the night shift attempted to restart a pump that had been shut down for maintenance. Unknown to them, a pressure safety valve had been removed from the relief line of the pump and the blank flange assembly was not leak-proof. Communication failures at the shift handover earlier in the evening, together with a breakdown of the rig's permit-to-work system, led to the disaster. Additionally, emergency procedures required platform personnel to muster in the gallery area; this was directly in line with the ensuing fireball and many people died. The survivors were largely those people who deviated from the mustering instructions – which did not address what to do if the mustering point was itself at risk.

There had been three visits from an inspector in the Department of Energy's Safety Directorate in the preceding year. The first was a routine inspection, requiring no immediate action. The second followed a fatal accident and identified weaknesses in those shift handovers and the permit-to-work system. The third took place ten days before the disaster and concentrated on areas in which construction work was taking place. That report accepted that the weaknesses in the second report had been 'tidied up', even though deficiencies in these areas were eventually found to be major causes of the disaster. This inspection took ten hours, was based on an ineffective sampling approach and failed to spot many of the factors which contributed to the fatal events. The subsequent enquiry concluded that the inspections were superficial to the point of being little use.

What this and other similar disasters tell us is that thoughtlessness is not a trivial thing, even though – as a word – it sounds as though it is.

HERE'S AN IDEA FOR YOU...

Imagine if a colleague was thoughtless or failed to put the requisite effort into an important task. How would you feel? Now imagine that it was you being thoughtless. How would it make others feel? Understanding the consequences of thoughtlessness is one way to prevent yourself from falling into such bad habits.

40 PAST, PRESENT AND FUTURE

We would all probably enjoy life a lot more if we could just live in the present. The harsh reality, it seems, is that we rarely can.

Emerson believed that people could never be happy unless they lived, like nature, in the present. Unfortunately that was rarely the case, as if people weren't lamenting the past, they were trying to foresee the future. I guess it's easy for nature because it doesn't seem to care too much about time (or at least it never says so). But Emerson did have a point and it's to do with how we appreciate the present.

DEFINING IDEA...

He who controls the past commands the future. He who commands the future conquers the past.
~ GEORGE ORWELL

If you spend the majority of your time thinking about the past or worrying about the future you will not only fail to enjoy the present but will also fail to appreciate the world around you. For example, how many of us get the Sunday afternoon blues because we worry about what we might face at work on Monday morning? And how many of us live our lives with a succession of 'if only I had the time...' moans? In both cases we tie ourselves in knots, which achieves very little. Although it would be nice to only focus on the present, it would be equally problematic – life would be a succession of surprises, both good and bad. So taking Emerson's advice literally isn't such a good idea. However, it does suggest that we need to balance our focus on the past and future, with being alive to what's present and fully engaged in 'now'. And the thing is, he's right – that's a lot more enjoyable.

From a purely metaphysical perspective, time is merely a succession of 'presents'. In other words there is no past or future, just lots and lots of nows. That's all well and good, but as human beings we appear to have a heightened sense of time because our lives are finite and we know it. No matter how long we might live, we all die, and it is fair to say that few of us would want to live forever anyway. That said, most of us would like to live long enough to realise our potential and fulfil our dreams, and I believe that a finite existence adds meaning to these and makes life worth living. This focus on time not only means that we care about our past and worry about our future, but it also ensures that a sense of time travels with us throughout our lives, from childhood through to old age. I remember my summer holidays as a child seemingly lasting forever and yet now, as a forty something, they are over in an instant. We spend ages getting nostalgic about our school days and at the same time fret about what we will be doing next week or when we no longer need to work. In that sense, at least, time can be a real pain; we can't ignore it.

HERE'S AN IDEA FOR YOU...

Log how much of your time you spend thinking about the past and the future. Do you think it is stopping you from being present to what is present? Practise being more engaged in the moment, really observing what's going on around you or listening intently to the person talking to you.

41 WE MUST GO IT ALONE

If being self-reliant means being able to stand on your own two feet, then leaving home or setting up your own business is a sure-fire way to prove that you can.

DEFINING IDEA...

Don't be disquieted in time of adversity. Be firm with dignity and self-reliant with vigour.
~ MADAME CHIANG KAI-SHEK

One of the many things which sets humans aside from the rest of the animal kingdom is the length of time it takes for us to mature. Most newborns in the animal kingdom are expected to fend for themselves pretty much from the moment they enter the world, but we hang around the family for at least sixteen years. One of the reasons is because of the time it takes for our brain to fully develop, although there may be many other reasons, such as wonderful home cooking. If you were anything like me when I was growing up, it certainly felt like a very long time. I was desperate to stand on my own two feet, so going to university was the escape route I needed. Today many adolescents don't seem to want to fend for themselves until they are in their late twenties and some come home after completing their studies. But there still comes a time when they have to cut themselves free of the family and go it alone.

The same is often true of work and although many of us dream of doing our own thing or running our own business, most of us don't. It is easier to have the safety net of a large corporation behind you which not only gives you the security of a salary, but also guides you in your career and provides the rules and processes which you follow every day. In some respects, working for a corporation is very much like being at home; there is only limited scope for self-reliance. Even so, there usually comes a time in your career when it is good to go it alone and cut yourself free of the mother ship.

Paul Theakston did this in 1987. Theakston's had been a family-run business for six generations and, like many independent breweries, they were a target for the big boys. After lots of acrimonious family rows, the brewery was finally sold to Scottish & Newcastle in 1987, one of the largest brewers in the UK. Although Paul Theakston was offered a role at Scottish & Newcastle, he decided that it wasn't for him and instead retained his independence by launching a new brewery which he named The Black Sheep Brewery (I guess you can see why). The experience of losing the family business was bitter, and one that has fortunately been tempered through the success of the new business which he has built up over the intervening sixteen years.

We all have to go it alone at least once in our lives, sometimes because we have to and sometimes because we want to. Such occasions allow us to show the world that we are truly self-reliant, which is a satisfying experience.

HERE'S AN IDEA FOR YOU...

Think about what makes you self-reliant. List those things which you have achieved through your own hard work and self-motivation. Seek to understand what qualities you possess that make you self-reliant and consider how these could help you 'go it alone' if you needed to.

42 THE POWER MEN POSSESS TO ANNOY ME

Sticks and stones may break my bones, but words will never hurt me – true, but only if you have the strength of character to stop them.

DEFINING IDEA...

No one can make you feel inferior without your consent.

– ELEANOR ROOSEVELT

At times I wonder whether Emerson was as cheerful as everyone made him out to be. His essays addressed some pretty interesting and often quite tough subjects and all of them had a slight darkness to them. Still, I think that tends to come with seeing the world for how it is rather than how you would like to see it. Whether or not he was of a happy disposition, he certainly didn't pack any punches. Men (and I guess women too) could easily annoy him, and reading Self-Reliance you can see that there were plenty of other things which also did – dead institutions and those who associated with them being just two. His remedy for avoiding the annoyance caused by others was the classic sticks and stones approach: in his words, 'No man can come near me but through my act'. Fine words and something we should all take to heart, but it can be difficult to do, especially for those of a more delicate disposition.

It is easy for people to annoy you, and those who are expert at it seem to have a sixth sense for both pinpointing the buttons to press and then pressing them. Emerson was of course right, as the power to let people get on your wick is entirely down to you and no one else. And, like the playground bully, if you stand up to them or just plain ignore them, they tend to go away and find someone else to annoy. Such people are called invalidators. Although there may be only a few malicious types who do it deliberately, most of us (and I do mean most) do it semi-consciously, either unintentionally or as part of the inbuilt defensive scripts we have developed over the course of our lives. What you have to remember is that most invalidators have inferiority complexes and, in order to make themselves feel better, either attempt to put other people down or control them. Dealing with invalidators so that they don't get to you means understanding the tactics they use to put you down. The key ones are uncertainty where they keep you on edge by not committing to things; projection, where they take their own feelings and put the responsibility for these onto another person's shoulders; generalisations and building you up before putting you down (just to make it even more unbearable for the victim). Invalidators tend to be both full of self-doubt and highly narcissistic – a frightening combination, but one which shows how fragile they really are. Ultimately, though, they can only be successful if you play the role of the victim, as this sets up a cycle of invalidation. Breaking the cycle requires that we all understand why we invalidate others, and also why we respond to invalidators so readily. Only then can we apply Emerson's excellent advice.

HERE'S AN IDEA FOR YOU...

In order to stop responding automatically you need to understand a bit more about yourself. Seek to understand what types of behaviour annoy you and determine why. Are there some unconscious reasons why you get annoyed? What can you do to stop yourself going onto automatic pilot?

43 WHOSE EXPECTATIONS ARE THEY ANYWAY?

Being self-reliant usually means breaking the unhelpful mental scripts drummed into us as kids.

DEFINING IDEA...

Do we not realise that self-respect comes with self-reliance?

– ABDUL KALAM, INDIAN PRESIDENT

Understanding what makes us the way we are is one of life's greatest quests, although at times it can feel like searching for the Holy Grail. It is, however, an important part of becoming self-reliant and for those who are willing to complete the journey, it's well worth it. We spend our formative years trying to please those around us – parents and school teachers when young; employers when adult.

Over time it becomes all too easy to be dominated and influenced by those around us and as a result we spend most of our life playing to someone else's tune. Emerson was very clear that each and every one of us has to break free from those who have influenced us in the past and attempt to influence us in our daily lives. In his view, we spend way too much time breaking ourselves on those around us as opposed to standing on our own two feet and being accepted for who we are. He has a point, of course, but to reach the stage where you can let the whims of other people wash over you takes time and is something that only tends to be possible later on in life. The reason why this can be so difficult is because most of our adult behaviour is ingrained into us at a very early age – as the Jesuit maxim goes, 'give me a boy until he is seven and I will give you the man'.

As a child you absorb the most from your parents although at the time you probably didn't realise it. It should come as no surprise to hear that parents are very powerful role models. Indeed, well-balanced parents can make excellent role models and produce well-balanced children, but the converse is also true. However, whatever your upbringing, you also develop coping mechanisms and internal scripts which help you get through your childhood and which typically end up ruling your life when you are an adult. These lead you to respond automatically to certain situations and people, and it is only when you grow up – and specifically when you reach middle age – that they catch up with you.

For example, those who were brought up in a strict environment, with perhaps a domineering mother or father who rarely offered them any praise, often grow up into perfectionists and workaholics. The internal scripts they have built are predicated on pleasing those in authority (their parents) and they take these into the workplace. Perfectionism is, in many respects, a shield that has been put up to protect the adult (and the child within) from being hurt by criticism and a lack of positive feedback. Eventually such scripts no longer serve us well and often end up being barriers to further success. We need to understand how they impact on us and either change or discard them. In Emerson's words, 'you have to be yourself'.

HERE'S AN IDEA FOR YOU...

Think about your childhood and formative years and try to understand what scripts you may have developed as you grew up. Ask yourself whether they are serving you well as an adult and which ones you might need to discard.

44 IF YOU CAN LOVE ME FOR WHAT I AM, WE SHALL BE THE HAPPIER

One of the things that we all crave is a desire to be accepted and loved for who we are.

Emerson believed that we should all be capable of loving people for what they are. Such a sentiment is fundamental to being able to get on with other people and, more importantly, to having a functioning and tolerant society. He also felt that if someone wasn't capable of loving him, he wasn't going to lose any sleep over it – also a valid point.

DEFINING IDEA...

The more you judge, the less you love.

~ BALZAC

I have been fortunate enough to have been happily married for well over twenty years. Although I am sure there are plenty of reasons why my wife and I have remained so close for so long, I think the principal one is because we love each other for what we are. And there is no doubt in my mind that we are happier as a result. We learned a long time ago to be tolerant of the little things that might grate occasionally and let them wash over us. We also learned to celebrate both our similarities as well as our differences.

When you think about it, that's what we all want – to be loved and accepted for what and who we are, warts and all. And yet as a basic desire it appears to be as elusive as ever. OK, we aren't living under the totalitarian regimes typical of the 1930s, but there are so many people and groups trying to force us to conform to their way of thinking that sometimes it feels that way. No matter on what dimension you choose to look at the world around you – work, family, religion, politics, economics, the environment – we see little by way of acceptance. What we do see, however, is lots of intolerance and a general myopia where it comes to accepting people for what they are. It's funny that on the one hand none of us like to be judged or told what we should be like, and on the other we're busy judging everyone and everything around us, hoping to bring them round to our way of thinking. Unfortunately, this is futile on every level; whenever someone has tried to force me into their way of thinking it has failed, and I am sure the same is true of you.

What we have to understand is that we are all unique and we all have our own talents, foibles and hang-ups. Just imagine how much better work could be if we could only cast our prejudices aside and accept our colleagues for what they are. Instead of being told that we have development points (often by someone who arguably has more), how about accepting that no one can become a Renaissance man or woman? It's far better to focus on people's strengths. This may be one of the greatest failings of Human Resources staff who, just like everyone else, like to pigeonhole and pretend that we can all become perfect workers. It ain't ever going to happen.

HERE'S AN IDEA FOR YOU...

The next time you're working with a colleague, focus on what their strengths are and see how best you can use them. A team will work better together and be more successful if everyone brings their strengths to bear on the task in hand – yours included.

45 DO WHAT YOU SAY AND SAY WHAT YOU DO

Many people you meet in life demand respect, but unfortunately they forget that they have to earn it first.

One thing that continues to fascinate me is why anyone wants to go into politics. Perhaps it's an ego thing or maybe it's because politicians like talking twaddle and never answering a direct question. Irrespective of why they do, it is a shame that the majority of politicians are not worthy of our respect.

DEFINING IDEA...

You do not lead by hitting people over the head – that's assault, not leadership.

– EISENHOWER

There are many reasons for this, but in the UK it's been the abuse of the parliamentary expenses system that has lost them much of their credibility and done irreparable damage to their reputation and to politics in general.

What is troubling is that when confronted by the press they usually fail to admit any wrongdoing and attempt to blame the system rather than their own greed. If it's not the system, they make some weak excuse that they've been too busy or are no good with numbers. Despite all this, they still expect the electorate to respect them. How can we, when it's patently obvious that many have been caught with their fingers in the till? We wrongly assume that because politicians are in high office they are whiter than white and have a solid moral compass. Otherwise how else could they fulfil their duties and set the standards and rules which we are all meant to live by? In my view, they shouldn't be there in the first place if they cannot.

The same is true of those who hold senior positions in the workplace. I always remember struggling to respect many of the partners at one of the professional service firms I used to work for. They, like the politicians, expected their staff to respect them and yet their moral compass was not just broken, but in many cases, beyond repair. I was at one with Emerson; I was more than willing to respect them but I was unwilling to pretend to respect them if they hadn't earned it. Had I done so, I would not only have been compromising my own position, but I'd also have been a hypocrite. Survival in these and indeed many other firms these days often comes down to your willingness to compromise, to lower your personal standards and turn a blind eye.

Earning someone's respect requires that you have what is known as congruence between your words and actions. When there is none, it is impossible to be respected. Congruence is about setting an example by walking the walk and talking the talk; doing as you would be done by. There is someone who does seem to be earning plenty of respect right now – Barack Obama. He not only maintained his congruence throughout the US election campaign, but continues to do so. Unlike so many politicians, who make empty promises during elections only to break them when in office, he started delivering on the promises he made right from taking the oath.

HERE'S AN IDEA FOR YOU...

How strong is your moral compass? Are you someone who commands or earns respect? Is there congruence between what you say and what you do? What can you do to ensure there is? Write down six to ten standards which you will live by and see how you do over a period of a few months.

46 THE DEBILITATING EFFECT OF FEAR

Throughout history we have been afraid of things, but today it feels like we are afraid of everything.

DEFINING IDEA...

One man calleth wisdome, what another calleth feare.

~ THOMAS HOBBES, SEVENTEENTH-CENTURY PHILOSOPHER

During medieval times, when people knew a fraction of what we do today, most of the population of Europe was afraid of the world around them and clung onto religion and pagan beliefs in order to make some kind of sense of it all. This fear of the unknown was very convenient for those in power, and the Church in particular, who were able to keep their citizens in check and maintain a degree of stability in society. Indeed, such was the level of fear that the world was going to end at the turn of the first millennium that there was a massive programme of church building when it passed without event.

Fear is a powerful emotion and its use as a tool with which to control our behaviour is well known. During the Cold War we were afraid of being nuked by the Soviets, and the governments of the day were able to use this to fund their wars across the world in order to keep communism in check. Today we are afraid of the impacts of climate change or being blown up by terrorists, and this fear is being used to change our behaviour once more. It seems that we all need a bit of fear in our lives in order to function.

But has it gone just a little too far? Today we appear to be afraid of almost everything. Parents are afraid to let their children out of their sight because they are worried that they might injure themselves and pubs have taken away the play equipment in their gardens because they are afraid they will be sued by the parents of kids who might fall off. Businesses are afraid to tell staff the truth about how they are not as good as they thought they were because the organisations are afraid that they might be taken to an industrial tribunal. The list is endless, but the results are profound. We are so busy being afraid of things, fuelled by the media, that we end up being paralysed as a society.

To break out of this futile cycle of being increasingly afraid of everything requires us all to have a better understanding of risk and probability. It seems to me that too many people believe that every risk has a high likelihood of impacting them. Naturally, this isn't true and we all would be better served if we applied a little bit of common sense and judgement to the supposed risks we face at home, at work and in general. Emerson was spot on when he said 'We are afraid of truth, afraid of fortune, afraid of death, and afraid of each other'. It's time we got a grip.

HERE'S AN IDEA FOR YOU...

What are you afraid of? Think about whether your fears are rational, or the result of what you may have read in the press or heard on the news. Consider a simple test – ask yourself how likely it is that the event (or risk) is really going to occur. Even if it does, will it actually affect you?

47 WITH THE EXERCISE OF SELF-TRUST, NEW POWERS SHALL APPEAR

Becoming truly self-reliant is one of the most empowering things you can do.

DEFINING IDEA...

That which does not kill us makes us stronger.

- FRIEDRICH NIETZSCHE

Emerson reckoned that those who relied on society to decide things for them were essentially weak. He believed that many of his fellow Americans were too willing to shun the rugged battle of fate where strength was born. Most fell at the first hurdle. He went on to compare and contrast the experiences of those who gave up too readily and those who just got on with things and toughed it out. The former he dismissed because he knew too well that after they had failed only once, they would spend the rest of their lives complaining about it and never bother to try anything again. He praised the latter, however, as these people not only got on with things (win or lose), but as a consequence enjoyed a much richer and more fulfilling life. In his view such individuals did not postpone life, but lived it; had not one chance, but a hundred chances.

The subtext of Emerson's opinion was that he believed that it was often those who had not had the benefit of a privileged upbringing who were the ones more willing to trust in their own capabilities. Perhaps so much was expected of the mollycoddled middle classes of Emerson's day that when they did not quite live up to their expectations they were classed as failures. The burden of expectation was too great for them to bear and the pressure placed on them by their families and the institutions of the day meant that many were set up to fail. Those who were not supported in any way had little choice but to learn to rely on their own abilities; there were no expectations to manage or live up to, they just got on with it. We see the same thing happening today, with the children of the middle classes having to live up to often ridiculously high parental expectations. And, as in Emerson's day, many have been set up to fail. Today, however, those who are unprivileged don't appear to have the edge that their counterparts did in Emerson's time; they often seem happy to live off state handouts. This is both bad for them and for society as a whole.

There is no doubt that trusting in yourself and your own capabilities is essential if you are to be genuinely self-reliant (ask any entrepreneur). Although, as Emerson suggests, it can be scary to do something for the first time, immersing yourself in a new venture can be incredibly character-building. What's more, after you have done it a couple of times, you begin to understand that you can trust in your own capabilities. And, given time and experience, this can develop into a virtuous circle where your self-trust and associated self-reliance encourages you to do new things and grasp new opportunities. It is truly empowering.

HERE'S AN IDEA FOR YOU...

Whose expectations do you have to live up to? Is it really necessary? Shouldn't you live up to your own instead? If you want to do that, then the best thing to do is to write them down and work out a plan which will allow you to meet them.

48 ANOTHER SORT OF FALSE PRAYERS ARE OUR REGRETS

In the final analysis Emerson's essay on self-reliance is a formidable self-help book.

The period in which Emerson was writing was one in which the early self-help gurus plied their trade, although certainly not in the numbers we see today. Some 693 million self-help books are sold every year and Americans, the most self-help-obsessed nation on earth, spend in the region of $8 billion a year on self-help in all its forms – books, seminars, DVDs and so on.

DEFINING IDEA...

Many of us crucify ourselves between two thieves – regret for the past and fear of the future.

– FULTON OURSLER,
US JOURNALIST AND WRITER

Although Emerson was very much a self-help guru, he was different to those of today. He fell into the 'tell it how it is' camp and was clearly someone who preferred his readership to pull themselves up by their bootstraps. In other words, he was a fan of hard work and earning your right to success. How things have changed. Today's self-help industry has been fuelled by the obsession with wealth and caters for the idle, people who hope that reading a book or attending a seminar is somehow going to provide them with the shortcut to success they seek. The subtext of all these books is that it's fine to be lazy and unwilling to work hard to achieve your goals, but somehow or other you still deserve to be rich and successful.

As Emerson favoured the tough love approach to self-help, he believed that regret was an unhelpful emotion. He figured that it was OK to regret calamities but only if you could help the sufferer. If you couldn't, you were better off attending to your own work and letting them get on with it. So instead of rushing to support those who would weep foolishly and cry for companionship, he would rather you imparted some home truths so that they could get back in touch with their reason. He believed that 'both gods and men welcome the self-helping man as for him all doors are flung wide, him all tongues greet, all honors crown, all eyes follow with desire. Our love goes out to him and embraces him, because he did not need it.'

It is true that those who can remain in touch with reason are respected and looked up to. A wonderful example of this is the microfinance movement. The concept is very powerful because it provides financing to the very poor in society and is a spur to low-level entrepreneurialism. Pioneered in the 1950s and 60s by Dr Akhtar Hameed Khan, a world-renowned social scientist from Pakistan who set up the Comilla cooperative programme, microfinance has proved to the world that it is indeed possible to provide credit to the poor of the third world. Although state aid programmes have their role, it is clear that providing the means to allow people to help themselves is highly effective – and is just the kind of self-help of which Emerson would have approved.

HERE'S AN IDEA FOR YOU...

Want to ditch regret? Try the following. First acknowledge why you want to let go of the regret. Next choose a symbol which represents it and make it real by drawing it on a piece of paper. Finally create a simple ceremony associated with letting go which involves physically destroying the paper. Such symbolism is very powerful.

49 SHAKESPEARE WILL NEVER BE MADE BY THE STUDY OF SHAKESPEARE

As an author, everyone always asks me if I am going to be the next J K Rowling. Of course not, I reply, how could I?

Of course I would love to sell as many books as J K Rowling, Stephen King or Dan Brown. But that's as far as I would go. I can never be any of these authors, as I am me and they are they. I might be able to learn some of the tricks of the trade from them but their unique talents are different from mine. I also have no desire to be any of them, or indeed write what they have written. I want to be known for my own writing, not as someone who is like another author.

Emerson makes a great play on being authentic and never imitating anyone and emphasises that none of us know what we are best at until we find out. In other words, to be the best at something or to be recognised for a great talent isn't something that can be taught; it just happens. As he points out when he mentions some of history's greatest geniuses, like Isaac Newton, George Washington, Benjamin Franklin and Shakespeare, no one taught them; there was no great master who directed them and honed their skills. It is also safe to say that they didn't attend a finishing school for geniuses either; they just became well known for the exceptional nature of their work. And to some extent there is always a little bit of luck because there is no tried and tested path to follow.

DEFINING IDEA...

...within his chemical limitations, whatever they are, each man has enormous possibilities for determining his own fate.

– ERIC BERNE, PSYCHIATRIST

I remember listening to an interview with Anthony Beevor, who has written some amazing books on the Second World War. Before he became well known for his ability to bring military history alive, he used to write trashy novels, none of which sold very well. He found his particular gift later on and probably only after he started to write non-fiction books rather than novels. And we mustn't forget that J K Rowling was once a poor single mum writing stories in a cafe as a means of keeping body and soul together and entertaining her child. It was only after a literary agent pushed the Harry Potter books that she and the whole Hogwarts thing took off. Plenty of other agents had rejected her manuscripts beforehand, and I'm sure they kick themselves every day for doing so.

What we have to remember is that we all have our gifts and talents and some of these are realised, but many are not. Our job in life is to find out what we are best at. This requires a combination of a belief in yourself (self-reliance in Emerson's view) and a desire to explore and experiment. You may be lucky to find them early on in life but, for most of us, it may take a bit longer and plenty of perseverance.

HERE'S AN IDEA FOR YOU...

Do you know what your unique talents are? Are you able to pinpoint your best ones? How do you make the most of them? Even if you don't exploit them in your daily work, is there any way you can do so in your spare time?

50 THE CIVILISED MAN HAS BUILT A COACH, BUT HAS LOST THE USE OF HIS FEET

In a world where it is easier to get in the car, maybe it's time to leave the keys at home.

DEFINING IDEA...

The real tragedy is that overweight and obesity, and their related chronic diseases, are largely preventable.
~ DR ROBERT BEAGLEHOLE,
WORLD HEALTH ORGANIZATION

Although Emerson did not witness the transportation revolution that came with the automobile, he could see the changes in behaviour that were occurring with the horse-drawn carriage. He believed that people had started to lose the use of their feet. But what he was really railing against was modernisation in general and its impact on society. He was of the mind that all the gadgets and technologies that were emerging even during his time were dumbing down individuals and making them lazy. Although I don't think you could necessarily accuse Emerson of being a Luddite, he did appear to have a negative view of technology, mainly we can suppose because it acted as a barrier to becoming self-reliant.

There is no doubt that technology in all its guises continues to change the world around us. Even looking back over the past twenty years, these changes have been significant. Take computers in the workplace. Twenty-odd years ago, when I started work, I was using punched cards and green-screen dumb terminals and now we have mobile Internet on the iPhone. I always wrote my reports by hand and sent them to the typing pool and now I write them on my laptop and print remotely; I used to do land surveys with theodolites and levels and now it's global positioning systems which give you your position instantly. Work has become easier. The home, too, has been transformed as domestic appliances and other labour-saving devices have eliminated much of the physical effort associated with running a house. Many of the changes have been good and we have all benefited from them. However, there is also a dark side.

As we have become more reliant on technology we have also become much more sedentary. We no longer need to move around as much as we did in the past and most of us spend our weeks stuck behind a desk, glued to a computer screen. We then get in our cars, drive home and spend all evening sitting in front of the television until we go to bed. The human body developed to be active and it's no wonder that we are all getting larger; obesity is endemic in many countries across the world. People in the US are getting fatter and fatter, and the population of the UK is the most rotund in Europe. We have also been dumbed down, as much of what we used to know has been subsumed by technology. People are no longer able to understand how things work; they just assume that they will. We may appear on face value to know a lot more, but we don't really, and very few people are willing to look at things in any real depth; we've become intellectually lazy too. Emerson would not be impressed.

HERE'S AN IDEA FOR YOU...

Break out of the habit of a sedentary lifestyle. Build some exercise into your daily routine and add a few mental challenges. It might involve walking to the station or cycling to work, and doing some Sudoku or crossword puzzles.

51 WHAT YOU ARE IS MORE IMPORTANT THAN WHAT YOU HAVE

In an age where what you have is more important than who you are, we are all guilty of failing to understand those around us.

DEFINING IDEA...

I'm all about breaking stereotypes.

– DADDY YANKEE, PUERTO RICAN SINGER

When Emerson penned his essay in 1841, he was concerned about the way people judged their fellows. He believed that most were too quick to judge someone by what they had rather than by who they were. The same, of course, is true today. Indeed, although I have written plenty of serious books over the past ten years, I have also dabbled a bit in humour. My first foray into this genre of writing was the result of a train journey when one of my fellow passengers really annoyed me with the incessant phone calls he made over the course of a forty-minute journey. Apart from the sheer banality of the calls, he insisted on speaking so loudly that the entire carriage could hear. So my book – Pains on Trains – dealt with all the annoying people you see on your commute. This was soon followed by Pains in the Office and Pains in Public, and I recently completed Broken Britain. All of the characters in the books are, of course, stereotypes and are based upon personal observations of the people I met every day. Although amusing to write about, stereotyping people is generally a bad thing because it fosters and promotes prejudice. However, it's important to remember that it is a natural function of the brain to do so because it gives us those all-important shortcuts that prevent our neurons from becoming overloaded with information.

One of the shortcuts we tend to use is what people have and own. For example, many of us assume that people driving around in Porsches or who own huge houses in the countryside are better than those who live modestly and refuse to buy into the consumer-driven culture. And we may believe that those who are wealthy are worthy of more praise than those who are poor. But what we own tells us nothing of who we are and, let's face it, displays of material wealth have until recently been easy for almost anyone; all you needed was an eye-watering mortgage, a bank loan or a credit card. Many people bought into materialism because they didn't want to be left out or be judged as being a nobody; they wanted to be accepted and to be someone. As we have become more materialistic we have become less interested in finding out about who people are, what makes them tick and what makes them unique and interesting. Hopefully the recession will put an end to the desire to judge people by their material possessions and, in any case, we should always remember that we can't judge a book by its cover. Dig a little deeper and you may find someone who is really interesting and worth getting to know.

HERE'S AN IDEA FOR YOU...

The next time you meet someone new (at work, or at a social event), do not judge them by what car they drive, where they live, or what clothes they wear. Suspend your judgements and seek to understand who they are – move beyond the superficial.

52 NOTHING CAN BRING YOU PEACE BUT YOURSELF

The hedonic treadmill drives our insatiable appetite for status and possessions. The problem is that it doesn't make us happy; only we can do that.

DEFINING IDEA...

If our position on the ladder is a matter of such concern, it is because our self-perception is so dependent on what others make of us.

~ ALAIN DE BOTTON, WRITER

Emerson concludes his essay with the following: 'Nothing can bring you peace but yourself. Nothing can bring you peace but the triumph of principles.' Although he was writing well over 150 years ago, this final statement sums up the importance of who we are to our general well-being. None of us can ever be truly defined by how much money we have, what we own or what position we might hold in a company or in society. Unfortunately we lost sight of this simple but important maxim as we embraced the consumer-driven, winner-takes-all messages that have been fed to us in recent years.

The problem is that we have allowed our obsession with money, power and status to define us and we now worry intensely about what other people might think of us – the classic status anxiety that the middle classes in particular experience. It has formed the basis of our lifestyles and our outward displays of wealth (the bigger car, the larger house, the fancier holidays) and has defined, or perhaps limited, our happiness and satisfaction as a result – mainly through the impact of the hedonic treadmill. This is the tendency for someone's economic expectations and desires to rise at the same rate as their income, resulting in no net gain of satisfaction or happiness; no matter what we've got, we always want more. The problem is that no matter how much we have it will never satisfy us; we'll always feel hollow inside.

It is now clear that money cannot buy happiness and our obsession with status does us no good whatsoever. Books such as Affluenza, Green with Envy, Shopped and the others that crowd the bookshops demonstrate that we need more than a life filled with cars, houses and iPhones to make us happy. It has been shown that people who buy top of the range sports cars only feel good as a result of their purchase for a few days at best. The same is true of lottery winners; most end up being no happier than they were before and many even become depressed and lament the day they won. In contrast, people who have suffered terribly in accidents (lost limbs, been disabled and so on) only experience a temporary reduction in their levels of happiness. After a few months they tend to be as happy as they were before their accident, even though life has changed irrevocably.

The lesson we can learn from this is that knowing who you are and being comfortable with your lot in life brings you far more peace than chasing goals which are defined by how much money you have, what position you hold and the size of your house.

HERE'S AN IDEA FOR YOU...

If you want to feel at peace go for a walk in the countryside and learn to appreciate your surroundings. Better still, do some sport as this releases serotonin which is so critical to the feeling of well-being. You don't need to spend lots of money on a new car to make yourself feel happy; just go for a run.

INDEX

Note: page numbers in bold indicate *Defining ideas* or *Here's an idea for you* sections.

Printed in Great Britain
by Amazon